BEAUTY AND THE BEAST

a fairy-tale thriller
adapted by

LAURENCE BOSWELL

NICK HERN BOOKS
London

in association with
The Young Vic Theatre

YOUNG VIC

BEAUTY & THE BEAST

A fairy-tale thriller

PRODUCTION
SPONSORED
BY DIGITAL
EQUIPMENT
CO. LIMITED

digital

FUNDED BY

LONDON
BOROUGHS
GRANTS
COMMITTEE

LAMBETH
ENVIRONMENTAL
SERVICES

LONDON
ARTS BOARD

THE YOUNG VIC THEATRE

In 1968 Lord Olivier and the National Theatre (then based at the Old Vic) talked of a theatre which would form a centre of work particularly accessible to students and young people. The theatre's programme was to include the classics, new plays, experimental theatre and educational work.

The Young Vic was established in September 1970 by Frank Dunlop and became the first major theatre producing work for younger audiences. In 1974 the Young Vic became independent of the National and went on to establish an international reputation for its productions, developing a wide-ranging audience of all ages and backgrounds.

In its 25 years the theatre has created an enormous range and style of work, from Beckett to Sophocles and Shakespeare to Lennon, including the professional world première of **Joseph and the Amazing Technicolor Dreamcoat** (Tim Rice and Andrew Lloyd Webber) and Arthur Miller's **The Last Yankee**. More recent highly successful Young Vic productions include Tim Supple's **Blood Wedding** by Federico García Lorca in a new version by Ted Hughes, the acclaimed **The Slab Boys Trilogy** written by John Byrne; a stage adaptation of four stories from Kipling's **The Jungle Book**; the enormous hit **Grimm Tales** for which Tim was awarded **Best Director – Off West End** by London's Time Out Magazine and which toured to Hong Kong, Australia and New Zealand; Martin Crimp's new version of Molière's **The Misanthrope** directed by Lindsay Posner; and a translation of Strindberg's **Miss Julie** by Meredith Oakes, directed by Polly Teale.

David Mamet's **American Buffalo**, directed by Lindsay Posner, will follow **Beauty and the Beast** at the Young Vic this Spring.

The Young Vic continues its commitment to creating adventurous theatre for as wide an audience as possible and particularly the young. As London's only purpose-built theatre-in-the-round and most adaptable thrust stage, the Young Vic offers unique opportunities for the exploration of intimate ensemble performance and the imaginative use of space, light and sound.

'Both the building and the stage/audience relationship are unique and altogether vital to the theatre scene of the metropolis' TREVOR NUNN

SUPPORT THE YOUNG VIC
BECOME A friend

'The Young Vic is a vital resource in London' PETE TOWNSHEND

'The Young Vic is a unique part of our theatre heritage' DAME JUDI DENCH

'The Young Vic audience offers proof that the theatre is alive in our time' ARTHUR MILLER

Join our Friends Scheme, and your support will immediately help the Young Vic continue to create outstanding, innovative theatre. Becoming a friend also enables you to join more fully in the life of the theatre by taking advantage of these excellent benefits:

friend | £20.00 annual subscription

- **Two half-price preview tickets to all Young Vic Company productions**
- **Regular advance information • Priority booking • Invitations to special Friends performances**

PLUS
- The **Young Vic Newsletter** featuring interviews with performers, directors and designers as well as inside information on Young Vic activities and events.

supporting friend | £50.00 annual subscription

- **Six half-price preview tickets to all Young Vic Company productions**
- **Regular advance information • Priority booking • Reserved seating**
- **Invitations to special Friends performances**

PLUS
- The **Young Vic Newsletter** featuring interviews with performers, directors and designers as well as inside information on Young Vic activities and events.

junior friend | £5.00 annual subscription

If you are under 16 years of age, become a Junior Friend for only £5.00 per year and receive:

- **Your own personal Young Vic card • Regular advance information**
- **Invitations to Junior Friends performances • The Young Vic Newsletter**

To find out more about the advantages of becoming a **Young Vic Friend**, or to join the free mailing list, call Philip Spedding, on 0171 633 0133, or pick up a leaflet in the foyer.

YOUNG VIC FUNDED TICKET SCHEME

It is central to the aims of the Young Vic Theatre to present adventurous work of the highest quality and so to attract younger audiences into the theatre. To this end ticket prices are kept to a minimum. However, the cost of tickets is still a major barrier for many people.

The Young Vic has introduced the **Funded Ticket Scheme**, appealing for funds to enable groups of young people to visit the theatre, almost always for the first time. During 1995 the scheme enabled over 2000 children and young people, who would not otherwise have had the opportunity, to experience live drama. In 1996, the generosity of our donors enabled the Young Vic to further develop the scheme increasing free theatre attendances to almost 3,000. Funding is currently being sought to continue the Funded Ticket Scheme.

The **Funded Ticket Scheme** is a unique venture encouraging audiences of the future. To find out more about the scheme please contact Philip Spedding, Development Manager, on **0171 633 0133**.

THE YOUNG VIC THEATRE COMPANY

13 February - 29 March 1997

YOUNG VIC
THEATRE COMPANY

David Mamet's

American Buffalo

Directed by Lindsay Posner

BOOKING NOW OPEN

THE YOUNG VIC STUDIO

The Young Vic Studio is dedicated to housing and nurturing experiments in writing, music, performance and design. It is an environment in which the encouragement of creativity and collaboration is the vital driving force.

The Young Vic Studio this Winter

The Studio schedule includes these leading innovative companies:

20 November - 7 December
> **PRIMITIVE SCIENCE** returns to the Young Vic to present ***Imperfect Librarian***, an intriguing and inventive story of a book with infinite pages.

11 December - 11 January
> **POP-UP** presents ***What About Me?***, for five-year-olds and under, to co-incide with our exciting production of Beauty and the Beast. A comic and touching story of a young person feeling left out, set in an imaginary polar landscape, rich in musical harmony and magical sounds.

14 January - 1 February
> **ACADEMY PRODUCTIONS** presents ***The Shift***
> Direction: Andy Lavender. Design: Andrew Fifield.
> Text: Clare Bayley.
> 1947, 1968 and 1997. Three years of change. Three generations of women on the verge of life-changing decisions who connect – or not – with that icon of female doom, the drowned Ophelia. A multi-media drama about making out and moving on, performed by six women.

11 February - 22 February
> **THEATRE PUR** presents ***Euphoria***, an unusual combination of oblique documentary, intellectual vaudeville and high technology, exploring the diverse means we have invented to probe, test, measure and manipulate the human personality.

To book tickets for all Young Vic Studio performances call the Box Office on **0171 928 6363**.

BEAUTY AND THE BEAST

The starting point of **Beauty and the Beast** is the family, with all its sibling rivalries, indulgent parents, spoilt children, economic problems and ambitions. Through Beauty's story, the Family goes on a journey which forces them to re-examine the materialism of their lives and to deal with the darkness and the splendours embodied by the Beast and his palace.

The Palace exposes Beauty and her father to the full range of human experiences, from extreme fear and despair to joy and elation. By the end of their journey they are more aware of the opposing elements which form them as human beings.
Laurence Boswell

LAURENCE BOSWELL – Director and Writer

Laurence Boswell trained at Manchester University where he was awarded the RSC Buzz Goodbody Award at the National Student Drama Festival. From 1990 until 1992 he was Associate Director at The Gate Theatre, Notting Hill where his productions included **Punishment Without Revenge** (Time Out Award) and **Don Gil of the Green Breeches**, and **The Gentleman From Olmedo** (Olivier Award for Spanish Golden Age Season,1992). In 1993 he became Artistic Director at The Gate and directed further acclaimed productions including **Bohemian Lights** (LWT Plays on Stage Award,1992) **Hecuba**, **The Cheating Hearts**, **Madness in Valencia** and **Agamemnon's Children**. More recently his work has included **The Painter of Dishonour** for the Royal Shakespeare Company, **A Voyage Round My Father** at the Oxford Playhouse, **Long Day's Journey Into Night** at the Theatre Royal Plymouth and Young Vic and Ben Elton's **Popcorn** at the Nottingham Playhouse. As well as directing, his publications include versions of **Damned For Despair** (LWT Plays on Stage Award 1993), **Don Gil of the Green Breeches** by Tirso De Molina and **The Painter of Dishonour** by Calderon De La Barca published by Absolute Classics.

BEAUTY
& THE BEAST

A fairy-tale thriller

Cast in alphabetical order:

Sherry Baines **Sister 2/Beast's Horse/Palace Chorus**
Liz May Brice **Beauty/Palace Chorus**
Simon Gregor **Brother 3/Warrior Prince/Beast/Palace Chorus**
Jonathan Hackett **Father/Palace Chorus**
Jan Pearson **Mother/1st Horse/White Witch/Palace Chorus**
Vicki Pepperdine **Sister 1/Beauty's Maid/Queen/ Palace Chorus**
Gary Sefton **Brother 2/Beast's Man/Palace Chorus**
Darren Tunstall **Brother 1/Palace Chorus**

Musicians
Nicholas Hayley, Mick Sands, Robert A. White

Directed by Laurence Boswell
Designed by Anthony MacIlwaine
Composer and Musical Director
Mick Sands
Lighting Designer Adam Silverman
Sound Designer John A. Leonard
Movement Lea Anderson
Assistant Costume Designer Kenny Ho
Assistant Director Isabel Hernandez
Research Sue Emmas

Production Manager Richard Howey
Company Stage Manager Anita Ashwick
Deputy Stage Managers Clare Norwood,
Chris Morrison
Assistant Stage Managers Helen Wallis,
Sam Rendell
Chief Electrician Paul Anderson
Deputy Electricians Mark Leahy,
Simon Macer-Wright
Stage Carpenter Nigel Parker
Costume Supervisor Alistair McArthur
Wardrobe Mistress Rachel Dickson

PRODUCTION CREATED BY THE STAFF OF THE YOUNG VIC COMPANY

Ladies' costumes by Karen Sharp and Dominic Young. Men's costumes by William Baboo and Frances Hill. Shirts by Emma Jealouse. Wigs by Jenny Adey. Dyeing by Clare Carter and Schultz & Wiremu. Shoes by Freed of London. Set by The Young Vic Workshop. Doorways by Streeter & Jessel. Lighting equipment supplied by Sparks Theatrical Hire, White Light (Electrics) Ltd., and Lighting Technology Ltd.

With thanks to: Persil, Comfort and Stergene, courtesy of Lever Brothers, for Wardrobe Care. Sue Mela and Hilary Philpot at the Royal Opera House. James Uglow of The Lion Troop. Kay Pratley for work with administration. Xanthe Vaughan Williams for translation work. Mark Richards. Elicia Cardenis

First performed at the Young Vic Theatre on **4th December, 1996**.

Play these games after the show

FROM RICHES TO RUIN

Beauty's family have lost their wealth. How many differences can you see?

There are 15 differences.

FATHER'S JOURNEY

Remember the story and trace
Father's journey.

In the tale he starts from his
cottage. What route does he take?

SHIP

COTTAGE

FOREST

PALACE

THE PALACE

Father reaches the Palace. Join the dots, what does he see?

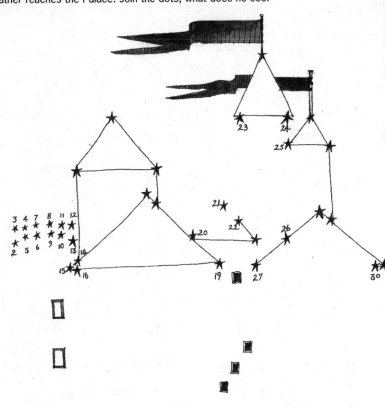

FROM BEAST TO PRINCE

(a board game for up to 6 players)

For the game you need a pair of dice and each player needs something small to mark their position as they move along the board. The aim of the game is to transform yourself from Beast to Prince.

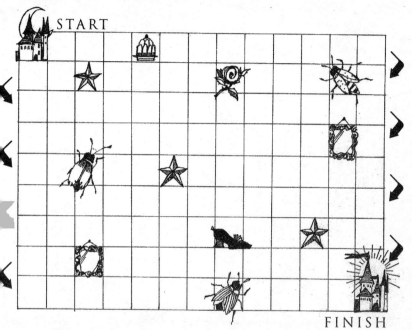

Start at the beginning and throw the dice to move along the board. Each roll of the dice has a different value, some scores are cursed by a magic spell from the Witch and you must suffer a forfeit, other scores are enchanted by the magic power of Beast and you get a special bonus! Whoever gets to the end first wins!

Remember, you must throw the dice and move the number of squares the dice shows you before the magic can take effect.

Score 2: move 2 squares, but Beast's Man has brought a feast, sit down to eat, and miss your next go **Score 3**: move 3 squares, yet don't trust your eyes, throw the dice again and have another go **Score 4**: move 4 squares, but Beauty's Father has taken a rose, he is Beast's prisoner, miss a go **Score 5**: move 5 squares, and Beast's horse gives you a ride, go forward five more squares **Score 6**: move 6 squares, but Beauty has not returned, lie down and miss two goes **Score 7**: move 7 squares, and send treasure to Beauty's Father, go forward two more squares **Score 8**: move 8 squares, and have a dance, move three more steps forward, but four steps back **Score 9**: move 9 squares, you are in Beauty's dream, go forward two more squares **Score 10**: move 10 squares, Beauty will not marry you, go back three squares **Score 11**: move 11 squares, you want to see Beauty, go backwards or forwards, to the nearest mirror **Score 12**: move 12 squares, but the Witch casts a spell, turn to stone until you throw a double **Hidden Magic** – If you land on a star ignore all other instructions but cast a spell and send one of your opponents back to the beginning of the game. If you land on a mirror double the score

BEAUTY'S DANCES

Beauty and the Prince dance in celebration, can you follow their steps?
A small arrow means a bunny hop and a large arrow means four steps forward,
always starting with your right foot.

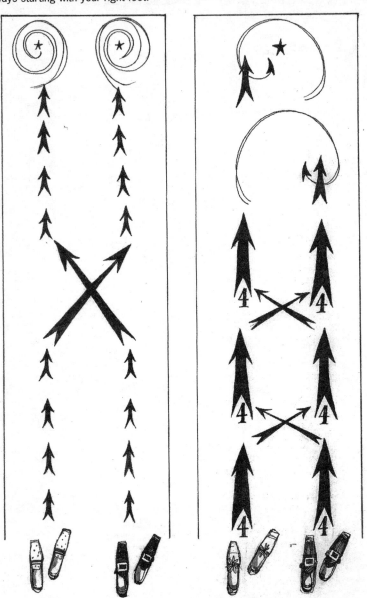

Games devised by Sue Emmas and David Thompson,
illustrated by Jessica Curtis and tested by the staff of the Young Vic.

BIOGRAPHIES

LEA ANDERSON – Movement

Lea Anderson is the founder of the dance company **The Cholmondeleys**. Productions for them include **Car**, which Lea also directed on video for Landseer productions, and **Flesh & Blood**. Other work includes **The Featherstone-haughs Go Las Vegas**, and **The Feather-stonehaughs' Big Feature**, **Khovanshina** for the English National Opera, Birtwhistle's **Mask of Orpheus** (Royal Festival Hall) and **Cabaret**, directed by Sam Mendes (Donmar Warehouse). Lea also wrote and presented the television series **Tights, Camera, Action** for Channel 4.

SHERRY BAINES

– Sister 2/Beast's Horse/Palace Chorus

Theatre includes the premiere of **Shakers** (Hull Truck), **An Ideal Husband** (Harrogate Theatre), **The Importance of Being Earnest**, **Daisy Pulls It Off** (both Manchester Library Theatre), **Tons of Money** (Derby Playhouse), **A New World** (Nuffield Theatre, Southampton) and **Agamemnon's Children** (The Gate, Notting Hill). Television includes **As Time Goes By**, **EastEnders** (both BBC). Film includes **Testimony** (directed by Tony Palmer).

LIZ MAY BRICE – Beauty/Palace Chorus

Theatre includes **An Ideal Husband** (Salisbury Playhouse), **The Lady of Pleasure** (Cambridge Festival Theatre) and **Cambridge Footlights**. Television includes **Chalkface** (BBC), **News At Twelve**, **The Worst Witch**, and **Coming Through** (all Central T.V).

SIMON GREGOR – Brother 3/Warrior Prince/Beast/Palace Chorus

Theatre includes **Weldon Rising & Inventing A New Colour** (Royal Court Upstairs), **Damned for Despair** (The Gate, Notting Hill), **Master Harold and The Boys** (Contact Theatre, Manchester), **Full Moon** (Young Vic/Theatre Clwyd) and **Good Person Sechuan** (Royal National Theatre). Television includes **Love On A Branch Line** (ITV). Film includes **Escape From Sobibor** (directed by Jack Gold), **Young Toscanini** (directed by Franco Zefferelli) and **Island On Bird Street** (directed by Soren Kragh-Jacobsen, to be released next year).

JONATHAN HACKETT

– Father/Palace Chorus

Theatre includes **One Flew Over The Cuckoo's Nest** (Manchester Royal Exchange), **The Alchemist** (Manchester Royal Exchange), **La Ronde** (Shared Experience), and **A View From The Bridge** (Manchester Royal Exchange). Television includes **The Advocates** (STV), **Middlemarch** (BBC) and **Poirot** (LWT). Film includes **A Man For All Seasons** (directed by Charlton Heston) and **Breaking The Waves** (directed by Lars Von Trier).

NICHOLAS HAYLEY – Musician

Nicholas started his professional career as a musician in theatre in 1976 at the London Palladium backing artists such as The Three Degrees, Sacha Distel and Shirley MacLaine. Other West End work includes various musicals, notably **My Fair Lady** in 1979 as orchestral leader. He also worked as sole musician for the Open Air Theatre, Regent's Park in 1986, and has worked extensively for the Royal National Theatre since 1978. Other work includes Symphony orchestras, recording sessions, films and international tours. Nicholas is also a professional instrument maker and restorer and has either made or restored the instruments he uses in **Beauty and the Beast**.

ISABEL HERNANDEZ – Assistant Director

Isabel Hernandez trained at the School of the Science of Acting as an actor and director. Her directing credits include **The Glass Menagerie**. Isabel was Assistant Director of the Young Vic's most recent production **Blood Wedding**.

KENNY HO – Assistant Costume Designer

Since graduating from Wimbledon School of Art in July 1996 with a BA in Costume Design, Kenny has worked on two feature films, **Diana and Me** and **Preaching to the Perverted**, both to be released in 1997. Other work includes various theatre and television productions such as Dennis Potter's **Cold Lazarus** (BBC & Channel 4), **Tommy the Musical** (Shaftesbury Theatre), and pop videos by Nick Cave, Julian Cope and The Divine Comedy's latest, **The Frog Princess**.

JOHN A. LEONARD – Sound Designer
John A. Leonard works consistently in the West-End, for most of the major British theatre companies, and in Europe and North America. Recent West-End work includes *Dead Funny*, *Passion* and *Company*. Other theatre includes *Faust* (Almeida), *Medea/Hamlet* (Almeida and on Broadway). Previous work at the Young Vic includes *Zenobia* (Young Vic/RSC), *The Jungle Book*, *The Misanthrope* and *Blood Wedding*.

ANTHONY MACILWAINE – Designer
Theatre includes *Agamemnon's Children* (The Gate, Notting Hill), *Dark Ride* (Soho Rep, New York), *Grimm Tales* (Leicester Haymarket), *Loot* (Magnificent Theatre Company national tour), *Cheating Hearts* (The Gate, Notting Hill and international tour), *Await The Tide* (Edinburgh Fringe), *The Lovers* (The Gate, Notting Hill and national tour).

JAN PEARSON – Mother/1st Horse/White Witch/Palace Chorus
Theatre includes *Grimm Tales* (Leicester Haymarket), *Paper Walls/The Sisters* (Scarlet Theatre), *Tantamount Esperance*, *Heredity* (both Royal Court Theatre), *If We Shadows* (Young Vic), *Imitation of Life* (The Bush Theatre). Television includes *Wycliffe*, *The Chief* and *The Bill* (all ITV). Radio includes *May and the Snowman* (BBC Radio 4).

VICKI PEPPERDINE
– Sister/Beauty's Maid/Queen/Palace Chorus
Theatre includes *Edward II* (Leicester Haymarket), *The Winter's Tale* (Theatre de Complicité), *The Day After Tomorrow* (Royal National Theatre), *The Atheist's Tragedy*, *Nothing Compares To You* (both Birmingham Rep), *Bedroom Farce* (Farnham Redgrave) and *Don Gil of The Green Breeches* (Gate Theatre). Television includes *The Bill* (ITV), *Friday Night Armistice* and *Saturday Night Armistice* (BBC).

GARY SEFTON
– Brother 2/Beast's Man/Palace Chorus
Theatre includes *A Midsummer Night's Dream*, *The Three Musketeers* (both Lancaster Promenade Season), *Mr A's Amazing Maze Plays* (Stephen Joseph Theatre Scarborough), *The Tempest*, *The Importance of Being Earnest* (both Bristol Old Vic), *Bad Company* (The Bush Theatre) and *Metamorphosis* and *Hobson's Choice* (both Birmingham Rep). Television includes *Peak Practice*, *Thief Takers* (both Central T.V), *Ghosts*, *Out of the Blue* (both BBC).

ADAM SILVERMAN – Lighting Designer
Theatre includes John Guare's *Moon Under Miami*, *Dark Ride*, directed by Julian Webber, *Bring in the Morning* (Apollo Theatre) and the New York Off-Broadway play *The New Bozena: Winter is the Coldest Season*. Opera includes *Faust* (Welsh National Opera), and productions at L'Opéra Français de New York and Long Beach Opera. After *Beauty and the Beast*, Adam will design *Tale of Two Cities* at the Gate Theatre in Dublin, followed by productions at Boston Lyric Opera, Seattle Opera and The New Israeli Opera in Tel Aviv.

DARREN TUNSTALL
– Brother 1/Palace Chorus
Theatre includes *The Sunset Ship* (Young Vic), *Hamlet* (Coventry Belgrade), *The Lovers* (The Gate Theatre), *The Recruiting Officer* (Manchester Royal Exchange), *The Comedy of Errors* (Bristol Old Vic), *Baldy Hopkins* (The Right Size) and *Cloud Nine* (Chichester Festival Theatre). Television includes *The Bill* (ITV). Film includes *Naked* (directed by Mike Leigh).

ROBERT A. WHITE — Musician
Trained at Guildhall School of Music and Drama. Robert is a composer, arranger, producer and multi-instrumentalist. His work includes productions for the Royal National Theatre, Royal Shakespeare company, English Shakespeare Co. and film, television and radio. Recent work includes *Fungus The Bogey Man* for BBC Radio (Sony Radio Drama Award).

THE YOUNG VIC COMPANY

The Young Vic gratefully acknowledges the financial assistance of the London Arts Board, the London Boroughs Grants Committee and the London Borough of Lambeth. Box Office sponsored by Digital Equipment Co. For the safety and comfort of patrons, smoking is not permitted in the auditorium. In accordance with the requirements of the London Borough of Lambeth persons shall not be permitted to stand or sit in any of the gangways. If standing be permitted in the gangways and at the rear of the seating, it shall be limited to the numbers indicated on notices exhibited in those positions. Photography or recording is not permitted in the auditorium.

Young Vic Company,
66 THE CUT,
WATERLOO,
LONDON SE1 8LZ.
A company limited by guarantee, registered in England No. 1188209.
VAT Registration No: 236 673348.
Charity Registration No: 268876.

Box Office **0171 928 6363**
Administration **0171 633 0133**
Press Office **0171 620 0568**
Fax **0171 928 1585**

THEATRE LISTINGS

GREENWICH THEATRE – Box Office: 0181 858 7755
6 Dec-25 Jan 1997
THE ADVENTURES OF HUCKLEBERRY FINN
31 Jan-15 Mar
OH WHAT A LOVELY WAR!

RICHMOND THEATRE – Box Office: 0181 940 0088
13 Dec-25 Jan 1997
Bonnie Langford, Bernard Cribbins, Chris Jarvis, and Terrence Hardiman in
ALADDIN
Richmond Theatre, The Green, Richmond, TW9 1QJ.

POLKA THEATRE FOR CHILDREN
21 Nov-8 Feb 1997
THE WIZARD OF OZ – For everyone over 6
Sponsored by Tullett & Tokyo Forex International Ltd

BEAUTY AND THE BEAST

To Carlotta, Myffanwy and Zinzan

Beauty and the Beast

Cast

(four men and four women, doubling)

1. Father
Narrator 7
Palace Chorus

2. Mother
1st Horse
White Witch
Narrator 6
Palace Chorus

3. Sister 1
Beauty's Lady in Waiting
Narrator 4
Palace Chorus

4. Sister 2
Beast's Horse.
Trunk 1
Table
Narrator 5
Palace Chorus

5. Beauty

6. Brother 1
Fire
Trunk 2
Narrator 1
Palace Chorus

7. Brother 2
Beast's Man
Narrator 2
Palace Chorus

8. Brother 3
Warrior Prince-Beast's Voice
Narrator 3
Palace Chorus

ACT ONE

1. Prosperity

BEAUTY's MOTHER *walks centre stage.*

The stage is bare except for a beautiful model 18th-century French city house.

And a full porcelain tea service.

As the family introduce themselves to us, it is as if we were new neighbours invited around for tea.

This whole section is a kind of dance. Formal and precise.

MOTHER. Long ago, in a city far away, there lived a merchant . . .

   Inviting FATHER – *a merchant – to join her.*

FATHER (*moving on stage, with great pride*). . . . who was so successful in all his business speculations that he grew enormously rich!

MOTHER (*ironically*). Which was lucky because he had six children! Three boys! And three girls!

FATHER. The oldest boy . . .

BROTHER 1 (*painfully embarrassed*). Was tall and shy.

FATHER. He loved to study.

MOTHER. He was always buried in some new hobby.

FATHER. His latest passion being . . .

BROTHER 1 (*with telescope*). Astronomy!

   Did you know, that the galaxy beyond the Milky Way, is 476 million light years away, and that you can see 5, 786 million other galaxies through this telescope?

MOTHER. That's enough now. Come and sit down. There's a good boy.

BROTHER 1. But Mama, I don't want to sit down.

FATHER. Don't disobey your Mother. (BROTHER 1 *sits.*)
There's a good boy.

FATHER. The Merchant's second son . . .

MOTHER. Loved all kinds of sport . . .

FATHER. He spent his days hitting balls and

MOTHER. Going on cross-country runs . . .

FATHER. He loved to . . .

BROTHER 2 (*climbing to some frighteningly high vantage point in the theatre*). Climb mountains.

MOTHER. Oh dear. Do be careful. Couldn't you come down now.

BROTHER 2. But Mama I don't want to come down.

FATHER. Don't disobey your Mother. (*He climbs down.*)
There's a good boy.

MOTHER. The youngest boy . . .

FATHER. Was dreadfully indulged by his Mother.

MOTHER. Now, let's make you look smart, young man.

MOTHER *is brushing the hair of* BROTHER 3 *and sorting - out his clothes.*

She doesn't hear the criticisms of the other male members of the family.

BROTHER 3 *is delightfully aware of what's going on.*

BROTHER 1. He's always being naughty.

BROTHER 2. But he never gets told off.

MOTHER. You must do up your top button or you'll catch cold dear.

BROTHER 3. But Mama I don't want to do up my top button.

MOTHER. All right then, darling. Never mind.

FATHER. The Merchant loved his sons.

MOTHER. But his pride and joy were . . .

FATHER. His three daughters.

SISTER 1. The eldest was devastatingly . . .

BROTHER 1. Conceited . . .

SISTER 1. Beautiful.

FATHER. She was also gloriously . . .

BROTHER 2. Spiteful.

SISTER 1. Intelligent.

FATHER. She was always top of the class because

BROTHER 3. She cheated in her exams.

BROTHER 1. And copied other peoples homework.

SISTER 1. She worked so hard. And read so many books.

FATHER. Her school report was full of . . .

BROTHER 1. Lies!

SISTER 1. Embarrassing praise!

BROTHER 2. Lies!

SISTER 2. And . . .

BROTHER 3. Complete . . .

SISTER 1. Admiration!

BROTHER 1. Nonsense!

FATHER. Well done darling. You are so so so clever.

SISTER 1. And beautiful.

FATHER. Yes yes yes of course.

MOTHER. The Merchant's second daughter was . . .

SISTER 2. Very different to her elder sister.

FATHER. She was less interested in her studies.

SISTER 1. She could hardly read.

FATHER. She was an elegant and refined . . .

BROTHER 1. Monster.

SISTER 2. Young lady.

FATHER. She was exceptionally . . .

BROTHER 2. Cruel.

SISTER 2. Gifted.

FATHER. As a dancer. She had a live-in ballet master.

SISTER 2 (*she does a little bit of ballet for us*). The other great passion of her life was . . .

SISTER 1. Vanity.

SISTER 2. Fashion.

BROTHER 2. Spending Father's money.

SISTER 2. And cosmetics.

MOTHER. The two eldest girls were either the very best of friends.

SISTER 1. Promise to be my best best best friend until you die!

SISTER 2. Of course my dearest dearest darlingest sister!

MOTHER. Or the worst of enemies.

SISTER 2. You are the ugliest stupidest . . .

BROTHER 1. Papa, they're rowing again.

SISTER 1. I will pull out your stupid liver . . .

BROTHER 2. Mama there's going to be a fight.

SISTER 1. And feed it to the cats.

BROTHER 1. Papa!

SISTER 2. I'm going to set fire to your hair!

> The GIRLS *launch themselves at each other and just as they are about to make contact we hear a baby crying. It is* BEAUTY. *She is represented as a bundle of silk in her* MOTHER'S *arms. The actress playing* BEAUTY *walks behind her* MOTHER *and makes all the relevant sounds.*

BROTHER 1. If the two eldest girls could never agree on anything for very long . . .

BROTHER 3. There was one thing which united them . . .

BROTHER 2. Always . . .

BROTHER 3. Always and forever . . .

FATHER. And that was the birth of the Merchant's third daughter.

MOTHER. Even as a tiny baby.

FATHER. The youngest daughter seemed so wise.

MOTHER. And so confident. The first word she ever spoke was . . .

BEAUTY. Beauty.

FATHER. Shall we call her Beauty?

SISTER 1. The eldest girls were absolutely furious!

SISTER 2. Papa, Beauty is not a proper name!

SISTER 1. I think she should be called crying blob!

SISTER 2. Crying smelly blob!

SISTER 1. Papa, can't we send her back now?

SISTER 2. Papa, why don't we have her adopted?

MOTHER. The Father's sons doted on their Mother . . .

FATHER. And worshipped their Father!

BROTHER 1. They listened in wonder to his tales of . . .

BROTHER 2. Dangerous and distant lands.

BROTHER 3. Where he bought and sold spices . . .

BROTHER 1. Silks . . .

BROTHER 2. And precious stones.

MOTHER. The eldest daughters had many admirers.

BROTHER 3. They gave themselves ridiculous airs . . .

BROTHER 1. Several wealthy merchants tried to marry their sons to the girls.

FATHER. They would not listen to their Father's appeals.

SISTER 1. Papa, I'll marry a Duke!

SISTER 2. Papa, I'll marry a Prince.

SISTERS 1 & 2. But not the son of a merchant!

SISTER 2. Oh no!

SISTER 1. Oh no!

SISTER 1 *and* SISTER 2 (*alternately*). Never! No! Never! No! Never! No! Never! No! Never! No!

This could go on for some time until . . .

Musical flourish.

MOTHER. The family lived in a beautiful . . .

FATHER. And expensive house . . .

MOTHER. In the centre of Paris.

FATHER. The house had been built especially for the Merchant's family. It was the envy of all their neighbours.

MOTHER. It had twelve bedrooms.

FATHER. And twelve servants, not including the two chefs.

MOTHER. And an enormous garden. But despite its size . . .

FATHER. And twelve servants and two chefs.

MOTHER. The eldest girls . . .

MOTHER. Were always . . .

FATHER. Complaining.

SISTER 1. Why can't we have a stable, Papa!

SISTER. Where is the indoor tennis court, Papa!

FATHER. But despite the little frustrations . . .

SISTER 1. We only have three fountains.

FATHER. And difficulties . . .

SISTER 2. We don't have a big enough ballroom.

FATHER. The family were happy.

SISTER 1. I'm not leaving this house again until we have an orchestra.

FATHER. In their own way.

MOTHER. The children grew up so quickly.

FATHER. And the Merchant's business flourished.

A dance section which expresses the family's thriving eccentric happy life together.

On the day of Beauty's fifth birthday . . .

A birthday song begins. Five candles burn.

BEAUTY. . . . her Mother died.

2. Ruin

The MOTHER *hurls the silk high in the air, a vocal flourish, the baby disappears and the teenage* BEAUTY *enters the action.*

BEAUTY (*looking at her* MOTHER, *whilst her* FATHER *covers* MOTHER *in a black silk*). My Mother loved me; she held me; she kissed me; and then she died.

The family watch a doll of the MOTHER *fly up from the real* MOTHER's *hands and disappear into the roof of the theatre.*

BEAUTY *sings a slow solemn ballad of mourning.*

This song is a counterpoint to the energy and growing frenzy of activity from the rest of the company.

BEAUTY *sings under all the following action, watching the place where her* MOTHER *disappeared.*

FATHER. The Father threw himself into his work.

The company reveal model ships which sail in increasingly tempestuous seas.

BROTHER 1. He spent recklessly.

FATHER. Buying new ships.

BROTHER 2. Invested foolishly.

FATHER. And investing in strange expensive cargoes.

SON 3. He made deals with dubious partners.

SISTER 1. And then a second tragedy struck the Merchant's family.

SISTER 2. Their beautiful house . . .

BROTHER 3. Burnt down to the ground.

> BEAUTY *picks up the doll's house. It passes through everyone's hands until it reaches* MOTHER.

FATHER. Everything was lost . . .

SISTER 1. The house . . .

BROTHER 1. The furniture . . .

SON 2. The account books . . .

BROTHER 3. Contracts . . .

FATHER. The exquisite cutlery . . .

SISTER 1. The library . . .

BROTHER 2. Toys . . .

SISTER 2. Ballet shoes . . .

BROTHER 1. A telescope . . .

FATHER. The beautiful tea service . . .

SISTER 1. The harpsichord . . .

SISTER 2. Family portraits . . .

BROTHER 3. The youngest son's new velvet suit . . .

SISTER 1 AND 2. And all the sisters' beautiful clothes!

ALL. Everything was lost.

> *The house is given to the* MOTHER, *who covers the house in red cloth.*

BROTHER 1. And then the Merchant's business collapsed.

BROTHER 3. Storms sunk his ships,

SISTER 2. Dishonest partners ran away.

SISTER 1. Taking all that was left of the Father's fortune . . .

FATHER. From wealth and comfort the family sank into . . .

BROTHER 3. Poverty.

> BEAUTY *begins to take off her smart dress and wig.*

This indicates their change of economic status.

The rest of the family slowly and unwillingly take up
BEAUTY*'s lead, the* SISTERS *last of all.*

All the CHILDREN *hand their model ships to their*
MOTHER *who covers them in a blue cloth, then leaves the*
stage.

BEAUTY *has been singing all this time.*

3. A New Home

As the family lose their smart clothes they look around at their
new surroundings.

FATHER. All that was left was a small derelict farm house.

He shyly produces a tiny wooden model of the cottage and
places it centre stage where the city house had been.

BROTHER 1. In the middle of a forest . . .

BROTHER 2. More than a hundred miles from the city of their
birth!

SISTER 1. The eldest daughters were completely horrified at
the prospect of living in such an isolated spot.

She mimes walking through a muddy field.

SISTER 2. Horrified at the prospect of farming!

SISTER 1. The girls wrote urgently to their fashionable friends.

SISTER 2. But received no replies.

BROTHER 3. Except one,

BEAUTY. Which suggested that all their misfortune was God's
judgment on their vanity and pride!

The SISTERS *grab the letter and rip it to shreds.*

FATHER. The family were too poor to employ servants and
even the eldest girls had to learn how to work.

BROTHER 1. The Father blamed himself for his misfortune.

Beauty's Work Song.

BEAUTY *sings as everyone is stuck in inertia.*

*By the final verse everyone joins in singing and working –
the* SISTERS *very unwillingly.*

FATHER *has risen from despair to begin work.*

The SISTERS *begin to work, but with great disdain,*
SISTER 2 *puts on wellies and tries to walk fashionably in
them.*

SISTER 2. How terribly improper to sing in a field!

BROTHER 3 (*in wicked parody*). What awfully bad manners to
be happy on a farm.

The BOYS *redouble their efforts and sing another verse of
the song with increased energy.* FATHER *works and*
BEAUTY *speaks over their singing.*

BEAUTY. But Beauty was not truly happy. In her heart she
still mourned the death of her Mother, and the loss of her
home, but she worked hard and smiled as she learnt about
bees. (*Mimes sting.*) and honey (*Licks fingers.*) and chickens
and eggs.

BEAUTY *produces an egg from her pocket and throws it to
one of her* SISTERS.

*More and more eggs appear and an elaborate and
dangerous egg-throwing routine develops between the*
CHILDREN *and finally even the* FATHER *joins in.*

BROTHER 1. After two years the family became quite settled
in their new home and in their new way of life.

SISTER 2. And then one day a letter arrived!

The final egg splatters on the head of SISTER 2 *thrown by*
BROTHER 3.

4. New Hope

MOTHER *delivers the letter.*

FATHER *opens the letter in silence, the* CHILDREN *gather around in expectation.*

FATHER. The letter contained good news! One of the Merchant's ships, which had been lost, was found:

'Your ship is standing in port with a rich cargo.'

An outbreak of mass joy; music, dance and hugging.

BROTHER 1. Thank God!

SISTER 1. The end of poverty!

BROTHER 2. Thank God.

SISTER 2. Back to the city!

BROTHER 3. Oh Father! Oh Father!

FATHER. Calm down children, calm down. 'PS. Come at once to prevent your dishonest partners from selling the cargo at a low price for a quick profit.' – I must leave at once!

BROTHER 2. But Father, the harvest!

BROTHER 3. We need you in the fields!

FATHER. When I repossess my ship, we can buy new fields!

SISTER 2. Can we go back to the city?

FATHER. Anything we want!

SISTER 1. Will you bring us back presents?

FATHER. Of course.

SISTER 2. A new dress from the Spring Collection?

FATHER. Anything!

SISTER 1. A harpsichord?

FATHER. Yes!

BROTHER 2. An iron plough?

FATHER. Two!

SISTER 1. A new library?

FATHER. Anything.

BROTHER 1. Leather boots?

FATHER. Six pairs!

BROTHER 2. A football?

FATHER. Yes.

BROTHER 1. A three-dimensional model of the solar system?

FATHER. Yes.

SISTER 1. A solid gold carriage pulled by six white stallions?

FATHER. Erm . . .

SISTER 1. Servants, maids, ladies-in-waiting?

BROTHER 3. And cleaners?

SISTER 2. And a beautician?

BROTHER 2. A pair of pistols?

BROTHER 1. A machine to measure the speed of light?

BROTHER 3. A machine for making ice-cream?

FATHER. Everything, you can have everything your little hearts desire!

SISTER 1. We have climbed out of the pit of poverty and back.

BOTH SISTERS. Into the lap of luxury!

Music ends.

SISTER 2. Why is Beauty so quiet?

FATHER. Yes, Beauty what can I bring you?

BEAUTY. Papa, just come home safely!

SISTER 1. Our little sister is trying to make herself seem virtuous with her humble request!

SISTER 2. How utterly spiteful.

SISTER 1. Sometimes I would like to cut out her eyes!

SISTER 2. I'd like to bite out her wind pipe.

FATHER. Now then dear daughters, less of your high spirits. Please, Beauty, for a girl of your age it's not natural, you must choose something.

BEAUTY. Please bring me a rose, Father.

FATHER. A rose. A rose for my youngest daughter. Certainly.
Now children, fetch me my horse, I must leave at once.

MOTHER *becomes a horse, the* BROTHERS *lead the horse
to the* FATHER *who mounts and rides quickly away with
much waving and good-byes.*

5. The Father's Journey

*Fast and furious gallop to the port, which is accompanied by
the full company in a passionate stamping step dance, full of
expectation and hope.*

The HORSE *stops abruptly and throws off the* FATHER, *who
switches mood instantly from hope to dissolution.*

FATHER. The Father did not receive the fortune he had
expected. His ship had arrived in port as the letter had
promised, but his former partners had repossessed the cargo
and sold it off cheaply for a quick profit. The Father took his
former partners to law to reclaim what was rightfully his.
And although he proved his case, the legal proceedings took
six months and the cost of the litigation left the Father with
nothing! His fortune had escaped him.

FATHER. To add to his troubles, as the Father began his
journey home a snow storm blew up.

The FATHER *remounts his horse and sets off for home.*
HORSE *and rider travel very slowly up steep hills and
down dangerous gorges in constant conflict with the
warring elements.*

HORSE. On the road, horse and rider were exposed to
merciless blasts of snow and wind.

FATHER. The Father thought he would die of exhaustion.

HORSE. The horse wished he had stayed in the stable!

FATHER. As they reached the edge of the forest night fell.

HORSE. They could travel no further.

FATHER. They were buried in the snow.

The Father believed that this night would be his last.

HORSE. The path had disappeared.

FATHER. They were lost in the forest!

HORSE. And then he saw an old hollow tree.

FATHER. He sheltered inside.

HORSE. The night was long.

FATHER. And the Father was hungry.

HORSE. And frightened!

FATHER. He was sure that he would die. The Merchant said a prayer for his children and prepared himself for death.

HORSE. As he drifted into sleep wearied with exhaustion and shaking with cold.

Noises of owls, wolves and frogs transforms into a chorus of birds.

FATHER (*opening arms*). The Father smiled weakly as the dawn broke, on a new day he never expected to see. He mumbled a hasty prayer to thank God for saving his life.

HORSE. He gave his horse an aching hug.

FATHER. Well, old nag we have lived to fight another day!

HORSE. But his happiness was brief.

FATHER. Snow had covered up the path.

HORSE. The horse could not keep its footing.

FATHER. They struggled on slowly not knowing where they were going, and then . . .

HORSE. At the point of complete despair, when they had given up all hope they saw . . .

FATHER. A beautiful palace!

6. The Palace I

This is the magical home of the BEAST.

No one has eaten or dreamt so far in the story, but as soon as we enter The Palace, people and animals eat, sleep and dream.

The magic of The Palace is generated by the company, who form The Palace chorus. The Palace is a constant synthesis of music, song and dance.

HORSE. Horse and rider move forward slowly in wonder.

FATHER. A long avenue led to The Palace.

HORSE. On both sides were orange trees.

FATHER. Covered in blossoms.

HORSE. And heavy with fruit.

FATHER. Blossoms . . . and fruit? . . .

HORSE. Said the Father, who was very confused.

FATHER. I'm confused.

HORSE. Where's the snow?

FATHER. Thought the horse, who wasn't confused!

HORSE. But delighted!

FATHER. But it's winter and how can there be both blossoms and fruit?

HORSE. Before he could continue his contemplations a stairway appeared.

The company form a stairway . At this stage The Palace is a mixture of gymnastics and dance.

FATHER. The stairway was decorated with diamonds and its banisters were made of gold.

The FATHER *runs up the stairway and jumps into mid air.*

The FATHER *begins to explore the many rooms of The Palace.*

To begin with the relationship between the FATHER *and the* CHORUS *is very tentative. The* FATHER *is nervous and afraid.*

He keeps trying to witness the moving walls of The Palace.

He keeps turning his back to try and catch the chorus out.

Then he gives up trying to control the situation and allows himself to become part of The Palace, part of the chorus, part of the dance.

As he begins his journey around The Palace the COMPANY *move about the stage in an elaborate dance, each holding a candelabra.*

The FATHER *moves across the rhythm and shape of the dance, delighting in the scale and riches of The Palace.*

The dance is sensuous and lyrical.

In the final movement of the dance the FATHER *falls into step with The Palace* CHORUS, *which finally comes to a gentle end leaving the* FATHER *centre stage. Tired but delighted.*

A CHORUS MEMBER *with a coal-scuttle speaks.*

THE FIRE. Tired of roaming through large empty rooms the Father stopped in a small but comfortable room in which a fire was burning.

The CHORUS MEMBER *sits down by the coal-scuttle and smiles at the* FATHER. *He warms his hands on this smile.*

FATHER. Perhaps this room has been prepared for me? (*He yawns.*)

NARRATOR 2. And with that he fell fast asleep.

The FATHER *drops to the ground from standing and is caught by two* CHORUS MEMBERS.

NARRATOR 3 (*throws the* MERCHANT *into the air*). If exhaustion drove him to sleep . . .

TABLE (*thrusting an empty plate under his nose*). Then hunger woke him up.

NARRATOR 5. On a table by the fire stood a plate full of food!

NARRATOR 2. The Father was confused again!

FATHER. Has this food been left here for me?

NARRATOR 6. As he had not eaten for more than three days, the Father's dilemma didn't last long.

NARRATOR 1. He hurled himself at the food and ate every last mouthful.

The FATHER *does this.*

TABLE. As soon as he'd finished one plateful another appeared.

Throws away the empty plate and receives another.

NARRATOR 3. Full of chocolate and cakes.

FATHER. When my host appears I must thank him for this breakfast!

The FATHER *dives at the new plate and somersaults us into another mood. The* CHORUS *begins another journey dance, similar to the first dance, but lighter and sharper, more irreverent. There is no music this time. A silent dance.*

FATHER. I must find my host and thank him.

NARRATOR 6. All the rooms were silent.

FATHER (*whispers*). Thank you.

NARRATOR 2. The Father was afraid.

FATHER (*whispers*) Thank you.

NARRATOR 1. He could find no one.

FATHER. Thank you.

NARRATOR 3. Not even a servant!

FATHER. Thank you.

NARRATOR 4. As he travelled through the Palace . . .

FATHER. Thank you.

NARRATOR 6. Admiring the rooms . . .

FATHER. Thank you.

NARRATOR 6. Some of which were the size of football fields.

FATHER. Thank you.

NARRATOR 1. Some of the ceilings seemed to be made of solid gold.

FATHER. Thank you.

NARRATOR 2. On the floor of one room was a carpet . . .

FATHER. Thank you.

NARRATOR 2. Which was so deep piled . . .

FATHER. Thank you!

NARRATOR 2. That he could hardly walk upon it.

FATHER. Thank you!

NARRATOR 5. It was the deepest richest blue.

FATHER. Thank you.

NARRATOR 5. And just as the Father was wondering what such a carpet would look like in a soft shade of peach . . .

FATHER. Thank you.

NARRATOR 1. To his great surprise . . .

FATHER. Thank you.

NARRATOR 3. The carpet turned . . .

FATHER. Thank you.

NARRATOR 2. A delicate shade . . .

FATHER (*says nothing, but mouths*). Thank you.

NARRATOR 3. Of softest peach.

NARRATOR 5. Then the Merchant began to imagine . . .

FATHER. Thank you.

NARRATOR 4. That The Palace . . .

NARRATOR 1. And all its treasures . . .

FATHER. Thank you.

NARRATOR 2. Belonged to him!

   FATHER *silent and still.*

NARRATOR 3. How happy this made him.

The dance stops completely.

FATHER. Even my two eldest daughters would be happy to live here!

Then the FATHER runs about The Palace proprietorially. In the third dance he is confident and bullish, leading the dance. The dance is very fast and dangerous with some stamping reflecting the FATHER's fantasies of wealth and power. During the dance he touches as much of The Palace and its treasures as he can. He gets out a note book and begins making an inventory of what he believes to be his new found possessions.

NARRATOR 4. He ran about The Palace making an inventory of all of the precious treasures he believed he now owned.

NARRATOR 3. The Father ran into the gardens of The Palace lost in his dreams of wealth and power.

The FATHER dances in the garden. He points at different flowers. He dances alone. The CHORUS watch in concern.

FATHER. Rare flowers.

NARRATOR 1. The Father was ecstatic!

FATHER. What gorgeous fountains.

NARRATOR 2. He felt like a man again.

FATHER. What topiary.

NARRATOR 3. Ready to impress his children once more.

FATHER. What statues.

NARRATOR 4. Ready to take his place again at the heart of the respectable.

FATHER. A river full of jumping fish.

NARRATOR 5. And fashionable society!

FATHER. I will bring my children to live in this paradise.

This palace which is mine, mine, mine!

NARRATOR 6. The Father burst into tears of joy. Tears of relief.

NARRATOR 1. And then he saw the rose bush.

The COMPANY *form a rose bush with thorns and one rose hidden in the centre.*

A strange primitive sound is heard, like a dinosaur writhing in some terrible torture. The MERCHANT *stops, sniffs the air, smiles and walks casually towards the rose bush. He puts his arm carefully into the bush to retrieve the buried rose when suddenly the bush explodes and the primitive sound escalates and we hear the word 'rose'.*

Holding out the stem of the rose is a strange creature.

The BEAST'S MAN.

He is a clockwork doll, he moves mechanically, constantly smiling and talks with a light jolly manner. BEAST *is not seen clearly on his first few appearances.*

We glimpse him behind huge doors or he stares down from the ceiling. Whenever he is near we hear loud primitive sounds which are on tape and the jangle of magical oriental bells, gongs and cymbals. For BEAST, *when he finally appears, will be a close cousin of a Chinese dragon. Huge, brightly coloured and terrifying.*

The MERCHANT *is crouched in absolute terror.*

BEAST. Who?

BEAST'S MAN. My master would like to know who gave you permission to steal his rose.

The FATHER *cannot speak.*

BEAST. Gratitude!

BEAST'S MAN. He lets you sleep and eat in his palace and now you steal his rose! He's very angry and he's going to punish you for your ingratitude.

FATHER. How will he punish me?

BEAST. Eat!

BEAST'S MAN. He will eat you!

FATHER (*in complete terror*). My lord!

BEAST. Flattery!

BEAST'S MAN. My master is not a lord. He is called Beast. And he hates flattery!

FATHER. Forgive me, please have mercy, I beg you, please. (*Grovelling for his life.*)

BEAST. Die!

BEAST'S MAN. My master is Beast, and he doesn't change his mind. He's going to eat you.

FATHER (*standing with all his courage*). I have a daughter called Beauty. I took the rose for her!

NARRATOR 4. And then the Father told Beast his whole sad story.

FATHER. I have six children, my wife died and my business collapsed. One of my ships was rediscovered but I was cheated by dishonest partners.

NARRATOR 5 (*critically*). Not forgetting to mention Beauty's request.

FATHER. I would never have dreamed of taking your rose but Beauty, my youngest daughter, asked. She wanted me to bring her home a rose. She insisted.

BEAST *makes a very quiet noise.* BEAST'S MAN *goes to* BEAST.

BEAST'S MAN (*comes back*). He won't eat you if you give him one of your daughters in exchange.

FATHER. That's impossible . . .

A terrible glimpse of self preservation flashes across his face.

What excuse could I give?

BEAST (*a terrifying mighty roar*).

BEAST'S MAN. My master says: 'NO EXCUSES!' The child must come willingly. Go now and see if one of your daughters will give her life for yours. You must return here in one month with the girl. You can leave her with us and then go, or can come back in a month alone, and be eaten.

BEAST. Escape!

BEAST'S MAN. Oh yes, and don't think you can escape because my master is very powerful, and if you don't keep your word he will search out you, and your children, and when he finds you he will eat you all!

FATHER. Beast, I will return!

BEAST. Promise!

FATHER. I give you my word!

BEAST'S MAN. That's excellent. Now, let me show you to your room.

FATHER. I want to go home.

BEAST. Tomorrow.

BEAST'S MAN. You can't leave until tomorrow. My master is very lonely, he loves to have guests to look after.

NARRATOR (*table*). So the Father went back to his room where supper was on the table and a fire burnt in the grate.

CHORUS *create exactly the same mood as before, but they reflect the* FATHER's *sadness, and try to cheer him up. The* FATHER *eats his dinner slowly, sadly, trying to resolve his dilemma. The fire shines bravely. A terrible noise shocks the* MERCHANT *out of his contemplation. A pause.* BEAST'S MAN *appears as jolly and mechanical as ever.*

BEAST'S MAN. Did you enjoy your supper?

FATHER. Yes, thank you.

BEAST'S MAN. My master would like to remind you of your promises.

FATHER. I will keep my word.

BEAST'S MAN. If you bring a daughter she must come willingly.

FATHER. Yes!

BEAST'S MAN. And she must know what will happen to her.

FATHER. What will happen to her?

BEAST'S MAN. My master will eat her!

FATHER. Yes.

BEAST'S MAN. You must tell her about my master, how frightening he is, how powerful, how ugly.

FATHER. Tell your master that I give him my word!

BEAST'S MAN. Sleep well tonight. In the morning a bell will wake you, there will be breakfast and then you may travel home.

FATHER. Thank you.

BEAST'S MAN. And here is the rose for Beauty. A present from my master.

FATHER. Thank you.

BEAST'S MAN *turns to leave.*

FATHER. Could I ask you something?

BEAST'S MAN. Anything!

FATHER. Are you human?

BEAST'S MAN. I am made of wood. The Witch made me to look after Beast's guests.

FATHER. Before he eats them ?

BEAST'S MAN. Yes.

FATHER. And who is the Witch?

BEAST'S MAN *says nothing.*

FATHER. Is she a good witch?

BEAST'S MAN. Yes.

FATHER. Why does Beast eat people?

BEAST'S MAN. Because he is Beast. Because he must.

FATHER. Do any people live here?

BEAST'S MAN. No.

FATHER. Your master must be very lonely.

BEAST'S MAN. Yes, he would like to get married.

FATHER. Does he want to marry one of my daughters?

BEAST'S MAN. Perhaps.

FATHER. Perhaps?

BEAST'S MAN. Or he might like to eat them.

FATHER. Why?

BEAST'S MAN. Good night, Merchant.

FATHER. Good night.

The FATHER *falls asleep. A bell rings, he wakes and eats breakfast.*

BEAST'S MAN. My master has a gift for you.

Enter BEAST'S HORSE.

FATHER. What a beautiful creature.

BEAST'S HORSE. I am Beast's Horse and I run as fast as the wind.

FATHER. But what about my horse?

BEAST'S MAN. She's safe.

FATHER. How do I ride such a Beast?

BEAST'S MAN. Just say to her, take me to where I must go.

FATHER (*mounts the horse*). Take me to where I must go.

They journey at great pace. FATHER *is terrified.*

7. The Return Journey

During the dance.

FATHER. Slow down. Slow down please!

BEAST'S HORSE *slows down.*

NARRATOR 1. On his way home the Father experienced many conflicting emotions.

NARRATOR 2. He was happy to be free of the Beast. And he looked forward to seeing his children.

NARRATOR 3. But he couldn't help thinking about the Beast. And his promise to return.

FATHER. What have I done?

NARRATOR 4. He thought about turning around and giving himself to the Beast.

FATHER. What use is a month?

NARRATOR 5. He was ashamed of himself.

FATHER. Oh God!

NARRATOR 6. For even thinking about sacrificing one of his daughters.

FATHER. I bet the Beast will eat my child whole. In front of me.

NARRATOR 1. But he could not help wondering.

FATHER. Would they make such a sacrifice for me?

NARRATOR 2. He couldn't help thinking . . .

FATHER. Which of my daughters would give her life for mine?

NARRATOR 3. He couldn't help hoping.

FATHER. I hope that one of them loves me that much! I won't ask them. It's not fair to even let them know about Beast's offer.

NARRATOR 4. Having made a decision he felt much better.

FATHER. They are only children after all. This is my responsibility.

I can't face my children with this news.

I will escape. I'll turn this horse around and ride away somewhere where Beast will never find me. Woa. (HORSE *stops.*)

The FATHER *tries to turn the* HORSE *but it will not change its direction. There is quite a struggle.*

Turn around horse, I order you, turn around!

The FATHER *loses the fight and surrenders to the* HORSE *which starts moving again towards the Merchant's home.*

FATHER. I just won't mention the Beast at all. I'll spend one precious month with my children.

I'll make sure that they can run the farm without me. And then I'll disappear without a word. I will go back to The Palace and Beast will eat me!

NARRATOR 1. And then the Merchant saw his home.

The HORSE *throws the* FATHER *off her back and disappears into the distance.*

8. Home Again

BROTHER 1. The Father was so deep in thought . . .

BROTHER 2. That he didn't notice his children . . .

BROTHER 3. Who had all stopped their labours . . .

SISTER 1. And turned in relief . . .

BEAUTY. And joy . . .

BROTHER 3. To see their Father . . .

BEAUTY. Who had been away for nearly a year.

They move towards him with great joy but stop suddenly as he looks up at the house in tears and smiles.

FATHER. My children!

SISTER 1. Father, what's wrong?

FATHER. Oh my little ones!

BROTHER 3. What is it, Father?

FATHER. A rose, Beauty! You asked for a rose!

Holding up the rose staring at BEAUTY.

BROTHER 2. Father, what's wrong?

SISTER 1. So she's the only one who'll get what she asked for!

SISTER 2. She's always been his favourite! What about my dress?

SISTER 1. And my harpsichord?

SISTER 2. My golden carriage?

SISTER 1. I hope you haven't forgotten my . . .

BEAUTY. Father, tell us what happened!

MOTHER. So the Father told them. He told of his journey to the ship.

BROTHER 1. An ocean-going clipper!

MOTHER. His dishonest partners.

SISTER 1. They sold it off cheaply?

SISTER 2. For a quick profit?

MOTHER. He told them about his battles in court.

BROTHER 2. The case lasted six months?

BROTHER 3. And you won!

SISTER 2. But the legal costs ate up all the profit.

SISTER 1. Oh no!

MOTHER. He told them of his night in the forest.

BROTHER 1. Poor Father!

MOTHER. He told them of the beautiful Palace.

BROTHER 3. Blossoms and fruit?

SISTER 1. Golden ceilings.

BROTHER 2. Rooms the size of football fields?

SISTER 2. Carpets that change colour with your thoughts?

BROTHER 3. Jumping fish!

The CHILDREN *all sit in wonder except* BEAUTY *who is very solemn.*

MOTHER. Then he told them about the rose bush and the rose. And then he told them about Beast.

BROTHER 1. He eats people?

MOTHER. And his promise to return in one month, alone, or with one of his daughters!

The CHILDREN *explode, all speak at once.*

BROTHER 3. We won't let you go back.

BROTHER 2. We'll kill this Beast.

BROTHER 1. We'll protect you, Father.

SISTER 1. It's all Beauty's fault.

SISTER 2. She's so horribly selfish.

FATHER. I have given my word. I must go back!

Again they all speak together.

BROTHER 1. I'll go in your place.

SISTER 1. She's killing our Father.

BROTHER 2. Let the Beast eat me.

SISTER 2. Why didn't she ask for a normal kind of present!

BROTHER 3. We won't let you go.

FATHER. Please be quiet, children.

BEAUTY. Father, this is all my fault. I asked for a rose. I will go to the Beast. I am happy to die. (FATHER *says nothing.*)

MOTHER. Her brothers tried hard to stop Beauty, but she was resolute. Her sisters felt that Beauty's offer was . . .

SISTER 1. The only reasonable solution.

SISTER 2. Privately they thought she only offered to go to gain attention.

MOTHER. Her Father said nothing! And, when the month had passed and it was time for Beauty and her Father to leave, a very sad parting took place.

9. The Father takes Beauty to the Beast

The FATHER *and* BEAUTY *stand outside the farm-house with the other children.*

BROTHER 1. Beauty could not speak to her Father.

BROTHER 3. She was so full of tears.

BROTHER 2. Her Father could not speak to Beauty.

SISTER 1. He felt so guilty.

FATHER. The Beast is frightening!

BROTHER 1. Beauty said nothing!

FATHER. He will eat you!

BROTHER 2. Beauty said nothing!

FATHER. We don't have to go.

MOTHER. Beauty said nothing!

FATHER. Beauty, I'll never be able to forgive myself.

BROTHER 3. Beauty said nothing!

FATHER. I've got a solution. Beauty, we'll run away together, just you and I.

Enter BEAST'S HORSE, *through magically opening doors.*

BROTHER 1. What's this, Father?

BROTHER 2. What a horse.

FATHER. This is Beast's horse. He must have been sent here to fetch us, Beauty.

BEAUTY. Father, it's time to go.

FATHER *unwillingly mounts the horse along with* BEAUTY *and prepares to leave.*

FATHER. Good-bye children.

Many good-byes exchanged, except from BEAUTY, *who is silent.*

FATHER. Take me to where I must go.

The FAMILY *create a wild and passionate journey dance, much faster and more furious than the first. They come to an abrupt halt and* BEAST'S HORSE *exits.* BEAUTY *and her* FATHER *and* FAMILY *are alone in silence.*

BROTHER 3. Then fireworks exploded all around them!

BROTHER 2. Illuminating the forest . . .

BROTHER 1. And revealing . . .

BEAUTY. The Palace of the Beast!

SISTER 1. Every room in The Palace was ablaze with light.

BEAUTY. The Beast must be very hungry . . .

MOTHER. It shone like a star in the forest!

BEAUTY. To give me such a welcome!

BROTHER 3. A thousand drums beat out a welcome!

BEAUTY. The preparations for my death . . .

FATHER. An artillery salute was fired!

BEAUTY. Are more splendid . . .

SISTER 1. Bagpipes screamed!

BEAUTY. Than the wedding of a Princess!

FATHER. Oh Beauty!

BEAUTY. You can eat me, Beast.

FATHER. Stop, Beauty.

BEAUTY. I'm not afraid . . .

FATHER. Come back.

BEAUTY. To die.

BROTHER 1. And despite her terror . . .

BROTHER 2. Beauty could not resist . . .

BROTHER 3. Running into The Palace of the Beast.

The COMPANY *form the stairway and* BEAUTY *runs and jumps into mid air, blackout.*

The Interval.

ACT TWO

10. The Palace II

BEAUTY *sits alone singing the ballad from Act 1.*

She has made a coronet of flowers and is weaving them into her hair.

As her song progresses a scene takes shape around BEAUTY.

The COAL-SCUTTLE *appears, sits and smiles; the* TABLE *arrives and produces a plate.*

FATHER *arrives and is just finishing a meal.*

The song is interrupted by a huge roar of . . . 'Beauty!'

Enter BEAST'S MAN.

BEAST'S MAN. It's time.

FATHER. No.

> *He wraps his arms around* BEAUTY.
>
> *Another roar . . . 'Quickly!'*
>
> BEAUTY *struggles to free herself from her* FATHER.

BEAUTY. I must go, Father!

FATHER. I won't let you!

BEAUTY. You gave your word to the Beast!

FATHER. He can take me. I can't let you go!

BEAUTY. But I asked for the rose. Let me go.

BEAST'S MAN. You must both come!

NARRATOR 1. Father and daughter . . .

NARRATOR 3. Walked slowly through The Palace to meet the Beast.

NARRATOR 2. Beauty was terrified, but she tried to smile.

NARRATOR 3. Her Father tried to hide his tears in his handkerchief.

NARRATOR 4. In her heart Beauty was saying good-bye to all her brothers and sisters.

BEAST. Good evening!

BEAST'S MAN. My master says . . .

BEAUTY (*interrupts*). Good evening, Beast!

BEAST. Beauty!

BEAST'S MAN. My mas . . .

BEAUTY (*interrupts*). I came of my own free will. And I know that you will eat me. My life is yours, Beast.

BEAST. Go!

BEAST'S MAN. You must leave.

FATHER. Beast, please don't hurt my daughter.

BEAST. Morning.

BEAST'S MAN. In the morning after breakfast a bell will ring, a horse will be brought, and then you must go home.

BEAST. Never.

BEAST'S MAN. Never think of this place again. You are forbidden to return.

BEAST. Gifts.

BEAST'S MAN. You will find two trunks in your room, fill them with gifts for your children. For your brothers and sisters. You may take any of The Palace treasures.

BEAUTY. Thank you, Beast!

BEAST. Good night.

BEAUTY. Good night, Beast.

BEAUTY *and* FATHER *remain.*

BEAST *and* BEAST'S MAN *disappear, the* FIRE *and the* TABLE *return.*

Two TRUNKS *are brought in.*

TRUNK 1. When they were back in their room . . .

TRUNK 2. Beauty's Father embarrassed his daughter and cried.

FATHER. Beauty, we must run away.

BEAUTY. There's no escape, Father. Now let's fill these trunks.

TRUNK 1. And Beauty and her Father collected all the most splendid dresses . . .

TRUNK 2. And valuable jewels . . .

FIRE. Which adorned The Palace . . .

TABLE. Breathtaking gifts for brothers and sisters . . .

TRUNK 1. When both trunks were full Beauty stopped and looked at her Father.

BEAUTY. We should empty these trunks and fill them with money. If my sisters are seen in these dresses, think of all the questions you will have to answer. If these jewels are to be useful to you, you will have to sell them. And how will you explain such enormous stones? Gold coins will be more useful. You can spend them when you want to and keep your wealth a secret.

TRUNK 1. So they emptied the trunks of dresses and jewels . . .

TRUNK 2. And filled them again with gold coins . . .

TRUNK 1. But the trunks were now so heavy they couldn't be moved.

FATHER. This is another of Beast's tricks. He seems to give me a fortune and then makes it so heavy I can't take it away. Beast is cunning.

BEAUTY. Don't be so sure, Father. Don't doubt the Beast. Let's close the lids and see what happens.

They close the lids and both drop instantly into sleep.

NARRATOR 4. They slept soundly!

NARRATOR 5. A bell rang!

NARRATOR 6. Breakfast appeared!

BEAUTY *and* FATHER *eat breakfast.*

NARRATOR 1. As they ate, Beauty's Father cheered himself up, thinking . . .

FATHER. Perhaps Beast won't eat Beauty at all.

NARRATOR 2. Beauty tried to cheer herself up thinking . . .

BEAUTY. Perhaps Beast won't eat me today.

NARRATOR 3. The food fed the Father's hopes.

FATHER. Beast did seem to like Beauty. Perhaps I can persuade Beast to let Beauty live and allow me to come here and visit her.

NARRATOR 4. Beauty's breakfast gave her courage.

BEAUTY. Beast liked me. If he doesn't eat me, then perhaps I can live with him in this Palace.

NARRATOR 5. And then a second bell rang!

Both BEAUTY *and* FATHER *stand bolt upright forgetting their breakfast.*

NARRATOR 6. The sound of the bell dissolved all their hopes.

BEAST'S MAN. It's time to go.

NARRATOR 1. The Merchant took a last look at his magical room and followed Beauty in The Palace.

NARRATOR 2. Father and daughter walked in silence . . .

NARRATOR 3. Beast's Man led them through a maze of corridors until they reached . . .

NARRATOR 4. A door which led to a stable.

NARRATOR 5. The horse stood waiting . . .

NARRATOR 6. With the trunks full of coins.

BEAST'S MAN. You must leave.

FATHER. Let us say good-bye.

BEAST'S MAN. Quickly.

FATHER. Beauty . . .

BEAUTY. Give my love to my brothers and sisters.

FATHER. I will.

BEAUTY. Go now, Father, quickly.

FATHER. Good-bye, Beauty!

BEAUTY. Good-bye, Father!

They embrace, then FATHER *leaves with the* HORSE.
BEAUTY *watches them go. She kneels in pain at their
parting and then falls to the floor. A* CHORUS MEMBER
covers her with a gold silk.

BEAUTY *is sobbing violently under the cover of the silk.*

The First Dream

NARRATOR 1. When Beauty's tears had stopped she fell
asleep.

NARRATOR 2. And dreamed.

NARRATOR 1. A bird flew through her dream . . .

NARRATOR 3. And then a young man appeared . . .

The WARRIOR PRINCE *enters.*

NARRATOR 4. And a magical woman.

NARRATOR 5. The young man was a warrior prince.

NARRATOR 1. And the woman was a witch.

BEAUTY *sits up, her face wet with tears. The silk is around
her shoulders.*

BEAUTY. Who are you?

UNKNOWN. A prince.

BEAUTY. And who are you?

WITCH. The White Witch.

BEAUTY. Can you help me?

UNKNOWN. Yes.

BEAUTY. How?

WITCH. Speak.

BEAUTY. Will I always be so unhappy?

UNKNOWN. No!

BEAUTY. Will I die in this palace?

UNKNOWN *stares at* BEAUTY *and gestures, but says nothing.*

WITCH. You had to come here.

BEAUTY. My name is Beauty.

UNKNOWN. We know.

BEAUTY. What is your name?

UNKNOWN. I am forbidden to tell.

BEAUTY. Then I will call you Unknown.

UNKNOWN *smiles.*

BEAUTY. And I will call you Witch. What shall I do here?

WITCH. Be patient.

UNKNOWN. Wait.

BEAUTY. And?

UNKNOWN. Be brave.

WITCH. And learn that we see with more than our eyes.

BEAUTY. What does that mean?

UNKNOWN. Don't trust your eyes.

WITCH. Don't say anymore.

UNKNOWN. Be patient, and don't trust your eyes.

The UNKNOWN *leaves the stage.*

BEAUTY. Who is that man?

WITCH *smiles but says nothing.*

BEAUTY. Will I meet him again?

WITCH. Yes.

BEAUTY. He seemed very troubled.

WITCH. Don't trust what you see.

BEAUTY. I'd like to help him.

WITCH. Then you must release him.

BEAUTY. How?

WITCH. He is a prisoner.

BEAUTY. Prisoner?

WITCH. But don't trust your eyes!

The WITCH *turns into a bird which flies out of* BEAUTY's *dream.*

BEAUTY *watches the* WITCH *leave and wants to say more.*

A CHORUS MEMBER *pulls away the golden silk.*

The COMPANY *form a magical clock which always wakes* BEAUTY *from her dream.*

NARRATOR 2 (*pulling the silk*). A clock chimed Beauty's name 12 times and she woke from her dream to find herself in a room full of light.

NARRATOR 3. There was a swing in her room.

NARRATOR 1. Which swung from a very high ceiling.

NARRATOR 4. There were soft carpets.

NARRATOR 5. And wardrobes full of clothes.

NARRATOR 4. Beauty chose a simple white dress.

CHORUS *throw* BEAUTY *the dress and the brush as she swings on the swing.*

NARRATOR 5. She brushed her hair and thought about her dream.

BEAUTY. Who was that man? Perhaps Beast has made him a prisoner in this palace and I have come here to set him free.

NARRATOR 1. Beauty found a knot in her hair.

BEAUTY. Ow!

NARRATOR 1. At which point something emerged from the cupboard.

It is BEAUTY'S MAID. *She is mechanical rather like* BEAST'S MAN.

BEAUTY. What are you?

BEAUTY'S MAID. I am your maid. The Witch sent me.

BEAUTY. The witch in my dream?

BEAUTY'S MAID. I am your maid. Shall I comb your hair?
  Here is a mirror.

BEAUTY. Thank you.

NARRATOR 2. Beauty looked at herself in the mirror.

BEAUTY. Don't trust your eyes. I don't understand.

BEAUTY'S MAID. What lovely hair you have.

BEAUTY. Thank you.

BEAUTY'S MAID. You should brush it more often.

BEAUTY (*laughs*). As Beast doesn't seem to want to eat me
  yet, perhaps I could look around The Palace.

BEAUTY'S MAID. I'll show you.

  The swing disappears. The CHORUS *take the brush and
  mirror from* BEAUTY *and her* MAID.

NARRATOR 3. Beauty followed her maid out of the room . . .

NARRATOR 4. And began her first adventure in The Palace
  of the Beast . . .

Palace Joys I

The COMPANY *start up The Palace dance which occurred in
Act 1.*

NARRATOR 2. She was very happy.

NARRATOR 3. She ran down long corridors full of sunlight . . .

NARRATOR 4. White silk curtains brushed against her face . . .

NARRATOR 5. At the end of a corridor Beauty saw a large
white door . . .

NARRATOR 6. She felt compelled to open it . . .

BEAUTY. Can I go in?

MAID. Of course!

NARRATOR 1. As she went towards the door . . .

NARRATOR 2. It seemed to open of its own accord . . .

NARRATOR 1. Beauty ran into the room . . .

NARRATOR 3. The walls were covered from top to bottom in mirrors . . .

The Room of Mirrors.

NARRATOR 1. Beauty saw herself reflected a thousand times.

The COMPANY *encircle her and each becomes a different reflection of* BEAUTY. BEAUTY *plays with her reflection. Turning quickly back, forward, dancing, and pulling funny faces.*

NARRATOR 2 (*handing* BEAUTY *a beautiful necklace*). Beauty found a necklace.

BEAUTY *takes the locket very carefully.*

BEAUTY. She turned around to speak to her maid. But she was nowhere to be seen.

BEAUTY. Inside the locket was a picture of the young man in her dreams. 'I will find where Beast has imprisoned you and set you free.'

Dance of Love in the mirrors – long enough to tire her out. She stops dancing, looks at the picture, looks at the mirrors and says:

BEAUTY. Don't trust your eyes?

NARRATOR 5. Beauty ran out of the Room of Mirrors and met her maid in the corridor.

BEAUTY. Where were you?

MAID. Waiting!

BEAUTY. Why didn't you come in?

MAID. The rooms are for you.

BEAUTY. Are there more rooms?

MAID. Follow me!

The MAID *and* BEAUTY *run down more corridors and stop outside another room.*

BEAUTY *reads from a sign which is high above the door.*

BEAUTY. The Room of Musical Harmony.

MAID. Go inside.

COMPANY *create Room of Musical Harmony.*

BEAUTY *plays in the room and then leaves.*

The room begins by echoing exactly any sound that BEAUTY *makes and then responds in harmony, finally generating a huge, shimmering, choral sound which combines many different melodies. The effect should be lyrical and overwhelming.*

MAID. Where now?

BEAUTY *closes her eyes and spins around. When her rotation is complete she points directly in front of herself.*

BEAUTY. This way.

NARRATOR 1. And Beauty and her maid set off down another corridor.

They stand in front of another door.

BEAUTY. Have you ever been in here?

MAID. Beast made all these rooms for you.

BEAUTY *runs into the next room which is:*

The Room of Portraits

BEAUTY. The room was full of paintings. The paintings seemed so real that Beauty wanted to touch them.

NARRATOR 6. Beauty saw a picture of a tree full of different kinds of fruit.

BEAUTY. Beauty reached into the picture and pulled out an apple.

BEAUTY *smells the fruit and bites into it.*

NARRATOR 2. It was the best apple she had ever tasted.

NARRATOR 2. And then Beauty saw a portrait of the young man from her dream.

BEAUTY. It looked so real . . .

NARRATOR 4. Beauty blushed . . .

BEAUTY. She wanted to kiss the young man in the picture . . .

NARRATOR 6. On the lips.

BEAUTY *moves slowly forward towards the painting. Just as she is about to touch the* YOUNG MAN *we hear a loud off-stage roar.*

BEAST. Beauty!!!

BEAUTY. She heard the roar of the Beast!

BEAST'S MAN. My master would like to see you . . .

BEAUTY. Of course!

BEAST'S MAN. In the dining room.

BEAUTY *follows* BEAST'S MAN *out of The Room of Portraits and into the dining room.*

A table is laid, but the room is empty.

BEAST'S MAN *offers* BEAUTY *a chair. She sits.*

As if by magic, doors open and BEAST *enters. He is terrifying.*

This is our first full view of him.

The WHITE WITCH *stands in the corner of the room invisible to* BEAUTY.

BEAST. Good evening Beauty.

BEAUTY. Good evening Beast.

NARRATOR 1. The White Witch stood and watched . . .

NARRATOR 2. She had made herself invisible to Beauty . . .

NARRATOR 3. But Beast knew she was there.

BEAST *gestures towards the food.*

BEAST'S MAN. Eat.

BEAUTY. Thank you.

BEAUTY *begins tentatively to eat.*

BEAST. Sleep?

BEAUTY. Yes I slept very well.

BEAST. Breakfast?

BEAUTY. Yes I enjoyed my breakfast, thank you.

BEAST. Today?

BEAUTY. I spent the day exploring The Palace. It is like a dream.

Beast, are you going to eat me?

BEAST. No! . . . (BEAST'S MAN *serves* BEAUTY *with a glass of wine.*) . . . Forever?

BEAST. Beast, your Palace is the most magical place I've ever known, but I can't stay here forever. I want to see my Father again and I miss my brothers and sisters.

NARRATOR 3. Beast recoiled in pain . . .

NARRATOR 4. It hurt him to know that Beauty was unhappy.

NARRATOR 6. Beauty changed the subject.

BEAUTY. Why do you speak so . . . simply, Beast.

BEAST *makes a groaning sound he is clearly embarrassed.*

BEAUTY. I don't mean to offend you, Beast.

BEAST. Fool.

BEAUTY. I don't think you are a fool, Beast. And the world is full of men who claim to be wise but who act like fools. And if you are a fool at least you have the sense to realise your folly.

NARRATOR 1. Beauty had eaten her supper. She was confident and relaxed.

BEAST. Song?

BEAUTY. Yes, Beast, I will sing you a song.

 BEAUTY *sings* BEAST *an old ballad.* BEAST *is clearly falling more and more in love with* BEAUTY.

BEAST. Frightened?

BEAUTY. Yes Beast, you do frighten me. But less than before.

BEAST. Am I ugly?

BEAUTY. Yes Beast!

 BEAST *is wracked with pain. The* WHITE WITCH *comes forward and catches* BEAST*'s eye. He calms down.*

WITCH. Ask her.

 BEAST *draws himself up to his full height, he is obviously bracing himself for some awful ordeal.*

BEAST. Will you marry me Beauty?

BEAUTY. Never Beast. Never! How could I marry you?

 BEAST *emits a deafening roar of pain. He is in agony. The* WITCH *signals to* BEAST'S MAN, *He rushes and opens a door for* BEAST *to rush out of.* BEAUTY *is left alone. Her* MAID *appears.*

MAID. What now?

BEAUTY. Back to my room.

NARRATOR 5. And so Beauty and her maid walked back to her room.

 BEAUTY*'s swing descends from above to indicate her room.* BEAUTY *wearily sits on the swing and the* MAID begins to leave the room.

MAID. Good night, Beauty.

BEAUTY. Good night.

MAID. Why are you so sad?

BEAUTY. I miss my Father and my brothers, and even my sisters.

 BEAUTY *swings on the swing and falls asleep.*

Dream II

The UNKNOWN *and the* WITCH *enter the dream. The* WITCH *pushes the swing and the* UNKNOWN *stands directly in front of the swing's path.*

BEAUTY. There you are.

UNKNOWN. Are you pleased to see me, Beauty?

BEAUTY (*stands on her swing*). Yes I am.

UNKNOWN. I need your help!

BEAUTY. I don't understand.

UNKNOWN. I am a prisoner!

BEAUTY. Where is your prison?

UNKNOWN. You can free me!

BEAUTY. Where is your prison?

The UNKNOWN *leaves* BEAUTY's *dream.* BEAUTY *is distressed.*

BEAUTY. Where are you going?

BEAUTY *jumps off the swing and runs towards the door through which the* UNKNOWN *disappeared, but the door is locked.*

WITCH. Beauty, remember to look with more than your eyes. (*Exits.*)

BEAUTY. Stop talking in riddles!

BEAUTY *returns to her swing. The dream ends. The clock chimes. The* MAID *enters.*

MAID. Breakfast.

BEAUTY. No. Thank you. I want to find this man. (*Shows the* MAID *the locket.*) Do you know where he is? He is a prisoner in this palace.

MAID *is silent and embarrassed.*

BEAUTY. Well I'll find him. I'll search every room in the Palace.

BEAUTY *runs very quickly out of the room, determined to find the* UNKNOWN.

NARRATOR 4. Then she looked at her locket and kissed it passionately.

Palace Journey Dance starts up. BEAUTY *is very strong and determined. She leads a passionate dance. Narration through the dance.*

NARRATOR. Beauty visited more rooms in search of the young man in her dreams.

BEAUTY (*reading above the door*):

The Room of Clowns

Dance changes into Room of Clowns. BEAUTY *enters a room full of* CLOWNS, *all of whom stand absolutely still.*

BEAUTY. Can you hear me?

CLOWNS *all shake their heads.*

BEAUTY (*confused*). If you can't hear me why did you shake your heads?

CLOWNS *look very sad but say nothing.*

BEAUTY. I don't want to play. I want to find this man.

BEAUTY *shows the* CLOWNS *her locket.*

CLOWNS *all study the locket intensely.*

BEAUTY. Do you know where I can find this man? He is a prisoner somewhere in The Palace.

CLOWNS *all look melancholically at the floor.*

Beauty was disappointed. She thought, 'What I need is a platoon of soldiers not a room full of silly clowns', and although Beauty only thought this and didn't say it out loud something terrible happened.

CLOWNS *all begin to march very seriously like vicious toy soldiers. Beating drums and playing bugles.* BEAUTY *is almost crushed by this barmy army.*

BEAUTY. Oh my God.

CLOWNS *very suddenly stop marching.*

BEAUTY. As soon as I wished they would stop, they did. Perhaps I can control this whole room with my thoughts.

CLOWNS *slowly break into devilish smiles.*

BEAUTY *looks at the* CLOWNS. *She is deliberately thinking of something. She has a big smile on her face.*

CLOWNS *all begin to fulfil* BEAUTY'*s fantasy.*

When BEAUTY *has satisfied her desire for play, she again freezes the room.*

BEAUTY. Will you come with me to look for this man?

CLOWNS *all nod their heads.*

BEAUTY. Then let's leave at once.

Music plays and the CLOWNS *follow* BEAUTY *out of the room and down the corridor.*

BEAUTY *picks up her maid and the troop travel around The Palace.*

BEAUTY *stops outside another door. She reads the name of the room.*

BEAUTY. The Room of Meditation. Let's try in here.

BEAUTY *heads towards the door but the* CLOWNS *don't move.*

BEAUTY *looks hard at the* CLOWNS *but they still won't move.*

MAID. They can't.

BEAUTY. Why not?

MAID. I can't.

BEAUTY. Are these Beast's orders?

MAID. No.

BEAUTY. Then whose?

MAID. The Witch.

BEAUTY (*pause*). The Witch. Who is the Witch? (*Silence.*) What has she got to do with the Beast? (*Silence.*) Can you tell me anything about her.

MAID. She made me.

BEAUTY. Did she make you? (*The* CLOWNS *all nod.*)

BEAUTY. Well, wait here.

CLOWNS *all nod. While* BEAUTY *enters . . .*

The Room of Meditation

This room is empty to begin with. Very gentle Indian music is playing. Very gradually, one by one, the room fills up with members of the PALACE CHORUS.

Some in yogic positions, some absolutely still, some engaged in Ti-chi. The atmosphere is exotic and peaceful. BEAUTY *enters the room and slowly examines the inmates of this most exotic place. She sits opposite the* CHORUS MEMBER *who is in the full lotus position and is silent.*

BEAUTY. I'd like to ask you a question.

Pause.

YOGI *nods.*

BEAUTY. I am searching for this man. Have you seen him?

All the CHORUS *slowly join in a collective movement which is graceful and sensuous. The movement reaches a climactic point.*

YOGI. We see with more than our eyes.

BEAUTY. That is what the Witch said.

BEAST. Beauty.

BEAST'S MAN. It's supper time.

BEAUTY *follows* BEAST'S MAN *out of the Room of Meditation. They leave the stage and as they re-enter they are at the supper table.* BEAST *enters. More peacefully.*

BEAST. Good evening, Beauty.

BEAUTY. Good evening, Beast.

BEAST. Eat.

BEAUTY. Thank you.

BEAST. How did you sleep?

BEAUTY. I dreamt of the Witch and the prisoner.

   BEAST *is silent.*

BEAST'S MAN. Salt?

BEAUTY. Thank you. Why do you not eat with me, Beast?

BEAST (*pained silence*).

BEAST'S MAN. Pepper?

BEAUTY. Thank you. Is it because you only eat people?

   BEAST *roars in agony.*

BEAUTY (*an outburst*). Beast, I don't understand you or your
   Palace. You provide me with servants and magical rooms
   and yet you keep me as a prisoner in this place. You seem to
   be gentle and considerate and yet I am afraid of you. You
   are a monster and you want me to marry you. I will never
   marry you, Beast.

BEAST (*an outburst of pain and rage*).

BEAUTY. Where is he, Beast? Where is your prisoner? This
   man. (*Shows* BEAST *the locket.*)

BEAST. Never.

BEAUTY. Tell me where he is Beast.

BEAST. Will you marry me?

BEAUTY. I have promised to set him free!

BEAST. Marry.

BEAUTY. I will never marry you, Beast.

BEAST. But Beauty I am . . .

   BEAST *is about to say something when the* WITCH *moves
   behind* BEAUTY *and puts a knife to her neck.*

BEAST'S MAN. The Witch.

THE WITCH. If you tell her now you know she must die.

BEAST (*backs away*). How long?

BEAUTY. Beast, come back. Beast.

BEAST'S MAN. I must follow my master.

BEAUTY. How will this end?

The swing descends and BEAUTY *falls asleep. Swinging.*

Dream III

UNKNOWN. Beauty. Why so sad?

BEAUTY. The Beast!

UNKNOWN. Yes!

BEAUTY. I cannot marry him!

UNKNOWN. Why?

BEAUTY (*upset*). Do you want me to marry the Beast?

UNKNOWN. Return love with love.

BEAUTY. But I love you.

UNKNOWN. Don't trust your eyes.

BEAUTY. I can't marry the Beast.

UNKNOWN. Free me from prison.

BEAUTY. I want to set you free. But you won't tell me where
    you are and I can't find you!

UNKNOWN. Beauty I am . . .

WITCH. Beauty's sleep was troubled.

The Big Dream

Knocking occurs at every door. BEAUTY turns terrified from door to door.

The doors fly open one by one. Sometimes it's BEAST, sometimes it's the UNKNOWN.

BEAUTY gives her locket a passionate embrace. The locket turns into the UNKNOWN and they dance passionately together.

BEAUTY. Do you love me?

WITCH (*appears in a doorway, BEAUTY screams*). Be brave, Beauty. Be brave.

BEAUTY. I am! I am!

All the doors close. BEAUTY's death lament for her MOTHER is heard. BEAUTY sobs. The Room of Mirrors returns.

BEAUTY sees herself reflected. The mirrors all reflect BEAUTY and follow her. Then they all start to be BEAUTY but not as BEAUTY is being.

BEAUTY stands still and watches, then she feels herself pulled into following her reflections. She is being manipulated by the mirrors.

There is a roar from the BEAST. The mirrors all disappear.

BEAUTY very slowly sinks to the ground as the work song is sung from Act One.

Then her FATHER appears with her three BROTHERS and two SISTERS.

They dance a gentle rather than lyrical dance in front of BEAUTY, her MOTHER is also present. The family dance out of the space backwards rather gently.

BEAUTY is exhausted. She sits centre stage. The dance has ended. The clock strikes. She is still for some time. And then she says very simply.

BEAUTY. Beast!

BEAST. Yes!

BEAUTY. I want to go home.

BEAST. Why?

BEAUTY. I miss my Father.

She breaks down.

BEAST. No.

BEAUTY. Beast, let me go. Only for a month. To say good-bye. I will come back. I will stay here with you forever.

BEAST. Nothing.

BEAST *is crying.*

BEAST'S MAN. My master can refuse you nothing.

BEAST. If you return in one month I will live. If you delay I will die. Here is a ring, when you wish to return, turn the ring so that the stone faces your palm and say: 'I wish to return to the Palace of The Beast.' .

BEAST'S MAN. Here are some gifts, Beauty . . .

BEAUTY. Thank you. Good-bye Beast.

WITCH. One month Beauty, or Beast will die.

BEAUTY *kisses* BEAST *softly and affectionately.*

The bell rings as if for morning. BEAST'S HORSE *is standing centre stage.* BEAUTY *climbs on the horse.*

11. Beauty's Journey Home

BEAUTY. Take me to where I must go.

BEAST'S HORSE. As Beauty travelled towards home . . .

BEAUTY. Older . . .

BEAST'S HORSE. Wiser . . .

BEAUTY. And very tired.

BEAST'S HORSE. She thought about the beautiful young man in her dreams.

BEAUTY. She thought about seeing her family again . . .

BEAST'S HORSE. She was very happy.

> BEAUTY *sings a song. The* HORSE *travels faster. The song is fast and passionate.*

> BEAST'S HORSE *stops and disappears.* BEAUTY *waves goodbye to the* HORSE.

12. Fatherly Advice

MOTHER *comes forward with the model of the farm and places it centre stage.* BEAUTY *watches with mixed emotions.*

BEAUTY. Beauty had not seen her home for two years.

FATHER. The sound of the horse's hooves drew Beauty's Father out of the house. He had just been going to shave, and his face was covered with soapsuds.

BEAUTY. When he saw his daughter . . .

FATHER. He stood very still . . . He had often dreamt of this moment and wasn't sure if it was really Beauty standing on the cobbles in front of him in the farm-yard.

FATHER. Beauty?

BEAUTY. Father!

FATHER. You're alive?

BEAUTY. And happy!

FATHER. The Beast didn't eat you.

BEAUTY. No!

FATHER. You've changed.

BEAUTY. Yes. (*They embrace, music.*)

FATHER. After an emotional reunion, Beauty and her Father sat down and talked.

BEAUTY. It was the best conversation Beauty had ever had with her Father.

FATHER. Beauty's sisters were in the city buying wedding dresses.

BEAUTY. Wedding dresses?

FATHER. Yes! And her brothers were working the land at the far end of the farm.

BEAUTY. So are we alone?

FATHER. Yes!

FATHER. On my journey home from The Palace, when I had left you . . . with the Beast . . .

BEAUTY. Yes.

FATHER. I wondered what I should do with all the gold coins that were in the trunks. I decided to hide this great wealth from your brothers and sisters. As I approached the farm and was wondering where to hide the trunks, I turned around and the horse had disappeared. Trunks and all. Beauty, I wasn't worried by the loss of the gold coins, I hadn't had them long enough for that, but the disappearance of the horse filled me with fear. It seemed like a bad omen. I thought the Beast had cheated me, and that he would certainly take your life. I was sure that you were dead. I went into the house, ignoring your brothers and sisters, and threw myself on the bed. In the morning as I was getting dressed I saw the two trunks, hidden in the wardrobe, just where I had decided I would hide them. I was so happy. This miracle seemed to prove the kindness of the Beast. I got on my knees and thanked Beast a thousand times, begging him to forgive me for doubting him and I resolved to change. All my life I have worked hard to make money. Why? To spend ostentatiously. To impress my neighbours. To spoil my children. To be thought a fine Father! I decided to hide the money and only spend it little by little when necessary on essential things. And since then I have used the Beast's money carefully. I have bought this farm and a little more land. I pay some of the local farmers to help us and so we have more time for ourselves. Your sisters have their music lessons again. Oh Beauty, each day since you've been gone I have hoped that the Beast would be kind to you. And every night I have feared that he had killed you.

BEAUTY. Although Beauty was pleased to hear how her family had lived in her absence.

FATHER. And delighted to know how much her brothers had missed her.

BEAUTY. She could not conceal the truth from her Father.

I'm not staying. This is just a visit. I'm going back to The Palace.

FATHER. Although this news distressed her Father he tried to be understanding.

I won't try and stop you from fulfilling your duty.

BEAUTY. It's not duty, Father!

FATHER. Beauty told her Father everything that had happened in The Palace.

BEAUTY. The Magical Rooms.

FATHER. No!

BEAUTY. The dreams!

FATHER. A young man?

BEAUTY. The Beast!

FATHER. Is kind!

BEAUTY. And look.

BEAUTY *opens the bag it is full of precious stones.*

FATHER. Beauty, you are rich! And although her Father was delighted by her incredible stories of adventures in The Palace

BEAUTY. They had difficult words about the beautiful young man and the Beast.

FATHER. We see with more than our eyes?

BEAUTY. Yes?

FATHER. Don't trust your eyes?

BEAUTY. What does it mean?

FATHER. The Beast appears to be ugly but his heart is good.

BEAUTY. Yes!

FATHER. And the young man is beautiful.

BEAUTY. So?

FATHER. Don't trust your eyes. Beauty, beware of that young man. Your dream may be a warning. Perhaps you should marry the Beast.

BEAUTY. How can I? He can hardly talk. Everyday the same silly conversation: 'Eat', 'Did you sleep well?', 'What have you been doing?'

FATHER. But Beast is no fool.

BEAUTY. But before his argument could go any further . . .

BROTHER 1. Beauty's brothers arrived from the fields . . .

BROTHER 2. They were overjoyed!

BROTHER 3. They hadn't seen their sister for more than a year!

BEAUTY. I am so pleased to see you again. How's the universe, brother?

BROTHER 1. Oh you know, continually expanding.

BROTHER 3. And then . . .

SISTER 1. Her sisters arrived!

SISTER 2. From the city!

SISTER 1. How charming to see you, Beauty.

SISTER 2. Delightful! (*The* SISTERS *move towards* BEAUTY *and kiss without making contact.*)

SISTER 1. As they were about to be married . . .

SISTER 2. They could not stoop . . .

SISTER 1. To any clumsy display of affection . . .

BROTHER 3. Which they didn't feel anyway . . .

BROTHER 2. Because inside they were still contorted . . .

BROTHER 1. With envy.

BROTHER 2. And spite.

BROTHER 3. And what they wanted to do most of all was not kiss her but . . .

SISTERS 1 & 2. Cut her to pieces.

13. Beauty's Dilemma

Family collage.

BROTHERS *chasing after* BEAUTY *to tell of their adventures and to hear her story.* FATHER *chasing after* BEAUTY *to try to persuade her to marry the* BEAST. *The* SISTERS *ignoring* BEAUTY *and trying to talk to their* FATHER *to talk about their weddings.*

The MOTHER *moving between them trying not to bump into anyone.*

MOTHER. Beauty enjoyed talking to her brothers!

BEAUTY. But she missed The Palace . . .

SISTER 1. Father, can we talk about my dowry?

MOTHER. Beauty had long and serious conversations with the Father!

SISTER 2. As soon as she comes back . . .

BEAUTY. But she missed her dreams.

SISTER 1. No one listens to us!

BROTHER 1. Her brothers marvelled at her new found independence . . .

BROTHER 2. And found a thousand ways to make her visit happy . . .

BROTHER 3. I've made a machine for making ice cream.

BROTHER 1. Would you like to see a lunar eclipse?

BROTHER 2. Let's play football.

BROTHER 3. But a month passed very quickly.

BEAUTY. Every morning, Beauty was determined to say good-bye to her family

SISTER 1. And every evening she could not tear herself away.

FATHER. On the day that Beauty was due to leave, a struggle took place.

The COMPANY *split,* SISTERS *on one side of the stage,* BROTHERS *headed by* FATHER *on the other.* BEAUTY *in the middle twisting and turning.*

SISTER 1. Her sisters made no secret of their desire for her to leave . . .

SISTER 2. It's been charming . . .

BROTHER 1. While her brothers implored her to stay.

BROTHER 2. Just a few days more.

BEAUTY. I promised Beast I would return in one month. I must keep my word.

SISTER 2. This news gave the eldest sister an idea.

SISTER 1. If Beauty breaks her promise to the Beast then perhaps he will kill her.

BROTHER 2. The sisters plotted . . .

SISTER 2. And so . . .

SISTER 1. Let's pretend we want Beauty to stay here with us . . .

SISTER 2. Yes . . .

BROTHER 3. The brothers were suspicious . . .

SISTER 1. And make sure she breaks her promise . . .

SISTER 2. And Beast will kill her.

SISTER 1. It's an awfully good idea . . .

SISTER 2. And we will be free of that horrible girl forever . . .

SISTER 1. Exactly. Dearest sister, please don't leave us.

SISTER 2. We will be heart-broken if you leave . . .

FATHER. They cried real tears.

BROTHER 1. The brothers were surprised at this sudden change of heart . . .

BROTHER 2. But as it stopped Beauty leaving . . .

BROTHER 3. For a whole week . . .

BROTHER 1. They forgot their suspicions.

FATHER. The Father was delighted.

BEAUTY. Beauty was unhappy. She loved her family but she wanted to leave. For the first time in a month she began to dream.

The FAMILY *disappear.* BEAUTY *lies down and puts an old blanket over her as if she is sleeping.*

14.   Beauty's Dream of Beast

BEAST. 'Beauty.' (*Very weak sound, far off.*)

BEAUTY. Why are you lying down Beast?

WITCH. Beast is dying!

BEAUTY. Beast, Beast don't die.

WITCH. You promised to return in one month!

BEAUTY. Beast, I'm sorry!

BEAST. Home!

WITCH. Beast wants you to return to The Palace!

BEAUTY. I'm coming!

FATHER. Beauty's decision caused diverse reactions!

Family collage II. Lots of criss-cross physical interaction. Everyone in the FAMILY *needing to talk to* BEAUTY *and other members of the* FAMILY *about* BEAUTY's *decision to leave.*

FATHER. Her Father broke into tears!

SISTER 1. Her sisters were delighted.

SISTER 2. Although they concealed their pleasure.

SISTER 1. Only saying out loud . . .

SISTER 2. Oh what a very fine sense of duty our little sister has.

SISTER 1. And well done, dear Beauty!

SISTER 2. Although they were a little confused.

SISTER 1. She is more than a week late. Where is Beast? She should be dead by now.

SISTER 2. Have a safe journey.

BROTHER 1. Her brothers were distraught.

BROTHER 2. They didn't want her to go.

BROTHER 3. Please.

BEAUTY. But I must go!

FATHER. Tomorrow, Beauty?

BEAUTY. No Father, now!

She shifts the stone in her ring around to face the palm of her hand.

Please take me to The Palace of the Beast!

The FAMILY *turn into the clock. They back off-stage singing the clock song. The swing descends.*

BEAUTY. I'm home!

BEAUTY'S MAID. Beast is very ill.

BEAUTY. Take me to him. (*They exit.*)

15. The Palace of the Beast III

BEAST *is lying down. Strange wheezing sounds.* BEAUTY *enters with her* MAID. *The* PALACE CHORUS *are watching. The* WITCH *is present.*

BEAUTY. Beast ?

BEAST'S MAN. My master is very ill.

BEAUTY. I know.

BEAST'S MAN. Beauty is here, master.

BEAUTY. Beast, I'm sorry I didn't keep my word. Beast, don't die, don't die.

Her MAID *gives* BEAUTY *a bowl of water and some flowers.* BEAUTY *washes* BEAST *and sprinkles flowers on the floor around him. She sings a short sad song for the dying.*

BEAUTY. Beast, I'm so unhappy. I didn't know how much I cared for you. I do not know what I will do if you die.

BEAST'S MAN. Beast is dead.

BEAUTY. No.

WITCH. You are too late, Beauty.

BEAUTY. I'm sorry.

WITCH. Beauty, what's in your heart?

BEAUTY. Regret . . .

WITCH. What do you regret?

BEAUTY. I wish I had come back sooner. I wish I could have thanked him for all his kindness.

WITCH. Do you love Beast?

BEAUTY. He's dead.

WITCH. Speak to him.

BEAUTY. Beast, I love you.

The PALACE CHORUS *begin a long slow chant. As they sing they seem to dissolve and melt away out of the doors.* BEAST *transforms from the monster into the Prince. Only* BEAST, BEAUTY *and the* WITCH *remain.*

BEAUTY (*takes the* UNKNOWN's *hands away from his eyes*). 'We see with more than our eyes.'

BEAST. I am the Beast.

BEAUTY. Don't trust your eyes!

BEAST. And I am the unknown. The young man in your dreams.

BEAST. Will you marry me?

BEAUTY. I will!

WITCH. The curse is broken.

BEAUTY. What curse?

Enter the QUEEN.

QUEEN. You cannot marry Beauty. You are a Prince. She is a merchant's daughter.

PRINCE. But, Mother.

BEAUTY. Please.

PRINCE (*running to his Mother's arms*). I must marry Beauty.

QUEEN. My son I'm sorry. You have your duty.

BEAUTY. Can you help us?

WITCH. This is a witch. When you were tiny she saw you in your cot and fell in love with you. She disguised herself as a beautiful Princess and offered herself as a wife.

QUEEN. Don't listen to her, she is evil.

WITCH. The Queen sought my guidance. As soon as I saw this Princess I knew she was a witch. I broke her spell and drove her from The Palace.

QUEEN. Be careful my son, she will turn you against me.

WITCH. She was furious and transformed you into a Beast. She cursed you with ugliness and she took away your power of speech. If she could not have you she wanted to stop you marrying anyone else. And then she killed your Mother for stopping the marriage.

QUEEN. I am your Mother!

WITCH. I challenged her curse and although I could not destroy it I added an antidote. You were to remain here as a Beast until a young girl should fall in love with you and offer to be your wife.

QUEEN. Dear son, don't believe this story.

PRINCE. You are not my Mother.

The PRINCE *draws his sword and stabs the* QUEEN, *who falls dead to the floor.*

BEAUTY. Is she dead?

PRINCE. Yes.

WITCH. No. You cannot kill a witch with a sword.

The QUEEN *stands up and is now clearly a cruel and evil* WITCH.

QUEEN. This battle is not over. If I can't have you no one else will keep you. (*She leaves.*)

PRINCE. Stay away.

BEAUTY. Will she come back?

WITCH. You must always be on your guard.

BEAUTY. Where is my maid and Beast's Man? Are they dead?

WITCH. They cannot die. They were never alive. I made them to look after Beast.

BEAUTY. Now I am free.

WITCH. Would you like your family to come to your wedding?

BEAUTY. Yes please.

WITCH *makes a gesture. Music plays and all three begin to dance.*

Doors open invisibly. slowly the family reappear one by one dancing in step with BEAST'S HORSE.

FATHER. And Beauty's family arrived.

BROTHER 2. They had no idea where they were.

BROTHER 1. Was that some kind of kinetic supra gravitational force, Beauty?

BROTHER 2. The brothers were over-joyed to see their sister . . .

SISTER 1. The eldest sisters were absolutely furious.

SISTER 2. We were in the garden picking flowers when we were dragged here by an irresistible force.

SISTER 1. It's completely inconvenient, Beauty!

FATHER. Who is this?

BEAUTY. And Beauty told her family the whole story of the Beast and the Prince and the Witch.

BROTHER 1. Her Brothers were amazed.

BROTHER 2. A wicked witch?

SISTER 1. Her sisters didn't believe a word of it.

SISTER 1. But they said nothing.

SISTER 2. Marriage was a very embarrassing subject for them at the moment.

FATHER. Both their weddings had been cancelled.

SISTER 2. Their future husbands had . . .

FATHER. Tired of their vanity and spite.

SISTER 1. And had simply called off the weddings.

SISTER 2. At a moment's notice.

BEAUTY. This man will be my husband, Father.

PRINCE. Do I have permission to marry your daughter, sir?

FATHER. With all my heart.

WITCH. And Beauty was married to the Prince.

For her sisters though, there was no happy end. They were turned into statues by a witch. They could still hear and see and feel, but they were to remain frozen in stone watching Beauty's happiness until they emptied their hearts of vanity, envy, spite and pride.

Wedding dance and song.

The End.

A Nick Hern Book

Beauty and the Beast first published in Great Britain in 1996
as a paperback original by Nick Hern Books Limited,
14 Larden Road, London W3 7ST in association with
the Young Vic Theatre, The Cut, London SE1 8LZ

Beauty and the Beast © 1996 by Laurence Boswell

Laurence Boswell has asserted his right to be identified as
the author of this work

Typeset by Country Setting, Woodchurch, Kent TN26 3TB
Printed by Cox and Wyman Limited, Reading, Berks

ISBN 1 85459 307 2

A CIP catalogue record for this book is available from the
British Library

Caution

All rights whatsoever in this play are strictly reserved. Requests
to reproduce the text in whole or in part should be addressed to
the publisher.

Performing Rights

Applications for performance by professionals and amateurs in
any language and in any medium throughout the world (including
excerpts and readings) should be addressed in the first instance
to Nick Hern Books, 14 Larden Road, London W3 7ST,
fax +44 (0) 181-746-2006.

No performance may be given unless a licence has been obtained.

Music and Songs

Companies wishing to perform the play with the songs and music
(by Mick Sands) used in the original production at the Young Vic
should contact Nick Hern Books at the above address.